LIFE WITH AN ALCOHOLIC

Turning Trials Into Triumphs

Virginia Crider

Cover Design:
David W. Miller

Christian Light Publications, Inc.
Harrisonburg, Virginia 22801

Christian Light Publications, Inc.
P. O. Box 1212
Harrisonburg, Virginia 22801-1212

ISBN: 0-87813-563-4

Printed in U.S.A.

Preface

This book grew out of my experiences as the wife of an alcoholic. I have known the pain, the heartache, and the hopelessness of life with an alcoholic husband, and I understand the fears, conflicts, and frustrations that the Christian wife of an alcoholic faces daily.

In counseling wives of alcoholics, I soon realized I could do little to help these desperate women. I could not step into their situations and cope with their problems. In each case these hurting women needed resources that would help them deal with their own set of circumstances.

My desire is to share the principles the Lord taught me as I sought to live a life that would honor Him while also living with an alcoholic husband.

— Virginia Crider

Table of Contents

Preface iii
Introduction vii
1. How It Happened 1
2. At Wit's End 5
3. Feed Bag Crisis 10
4. You Have No Right 14
5. Security—Where Do I Find It? 17
6. The Absolute Word 22
7. Pray—Without Ceasing 28
8. Fellowship 36
9. Submission—A Joy 43
10. What Can I Do? 52
11. You and Your Children 64
12. The Matter of Money 77
13. The Physical Side of Marriage 85
14. There Is Hope 89
Epilogue 92

Introduction

One day some years ago, the jangling telephone shattered the quiet in my house. The conversation that followed went something like this: "Virginia, you don't know me, but my husband is an alcoholic. Joyce [a mutual friend] suggested I call you."

My caller went on to say, "I am so ashamed of myself. Last evening I got so angry with Dick that I actually threw a bowl of hot lima beans in his face. Virginia, what am I going to do? I am a Christian and I know that wasn't right, but I get so frustrated."

This desperate person spoke also of her son and her hopes and fears for him. Whose influence would dominate his life—hers or his alcoholic father's? As I thought of my four children, that concerned me as well.

Most Christians live in a protected environment and understand nothing of the stress alcohol places on the family members of an alcoholic. Alcoholism can be devastating to the wife of the alcoholic. The responsibility of holding the family together and of being security for the children falls on her. Frequently she must cope with financial pressures that result from her husband's addiction.

Coupled with these burdens comes a staggering blow. Her husband may not appreciate her efforts, and he may even resent them. He may belittle her and accuse her of a multitude of wrongdoings. She may face constant threats to her physical and emotional well-being, along with actual abuse.

In view of the nature of alcoholism, only those persons who have experienced its effects can empathize with those who are going through similar situations. I lived with this condition for twenty-eight years. After struggling through the first ten years alone, I repented of my wandering and returned to the Lord in 1960. Then, praise His name, things changed.

This book is dedicated to those women who are caught in what seems to be an impossible situation, living with an alcoholic.

Virginia Crider
P. O. Box 326
Singer's Glen, VA 22850

1. How It Happened

How did I become the wife of an alcoholic?

Had anyone suggested to me as a teenager that I would marry an alcoholic, I would never have believed it. Me? No way! Why, look who I was! Look at my background. My family would not think of doing such a thing.

I am a descendant of a long line of Anabaptist believers who originated in Switzerland and Germany. My grandfather Showalter was a circuit preacher in the Virginia-West Virginia mountains during the early years of this century. Several of my uncles were ministers of the Gospel and one was a bishop.

Although the Lord never called my father to preach, my parents dedicated their lives to the Lord's work.

Each summer, from April through September, they bundled their four children into our old car—we were too poor to afford a late model—and drove to one of the churches in the highlands where they conducted Sunday school. When I was a baby, Mama set me on the classroom floor as she taught a group of children.

During those years Papa and Mama served regularly at two places—"back in the Gap" (close to home) and across the state line in West Virginia. This assignment consisted of two schoolhouses, one in Virginia and the other in West Virginia. We held Sunday school in the West Virginia schoolhouse in the morning, ate our packed lunch, then backtracked four miles to the schoolhouse in Virginia for the afternoon service. My future husband and his brothers sometimes attended Sunday school at the Virginia location.

Now let me explain how I fell into Satan's trap and

became the wife of an alcoholic.

Mama taught us to shun strong drink. She refused to use a much-loved family physician in our small town who had a reputation for using alcoholic beverages. Mama instructed us children when we delivered milk never to accept a drink from neighbors who used alcohol. "Don't even go into the house," she warned.

Then how did I become the wife of an alcoholic?

The year following my graduation from high school, I worked as the hired girl for a local Christian family. These children and I had attended school together, and one of the girls and I graduated in the same class. But nothing in my life had prepared me for what I was to experience.

My mistress expected me to go ahead without supervision from her, but I did not know how to "go ahead." Although I tried valiantly, it seemed as if I never could do anything quite right. A spot remained on a bedspread, or I missed some dust behind a dresser, or I failed to catch a cobweb trailing from the ceiling. If nothing like that happened, in my anxiety not to be clumsy I sometimes overreacted and chipped the plaster when dragging the vacuum cleaner up the winding staircase. How I hated that vacuum cleaner!

Toward the end of that nine-month period, I began literally to count the days and the hours until I could go home. Mama and Papa had no idea that I was so miserable. Mama told me later that if they had known, they would not have expected me to stay. For my part, it did not occur to me to quit.

The trials of that year kept me on my knees and in the Word of God. The next year Satan threw a punch I was not expecting and did not know how to handle.

A popular and sophisticated schoolteacher dropped in one day to see me. "Would you consider baby-sitting for Janie this year while I teach?" she asked. "I want someone who uses good grammar, and I know you do. I remember how well you did in my junior English class several years ago." Her compliment put me off guard. As she continued to exalt my character, I cast aside any reservations I may have had about the position and I accepted the job.

My employer treated me like family. She bragged about "my Virginia" to the other teachers, her personal physician, and her family. She even boasted of my Bible knowledge, small as it was then in comparison to what I have learned over the years since. I was blind; I did not realize what Satan was doing to me, using pride to set me up for a fall.

I cannot say at what point it happened, but I began to neglect reading my Bible in favor of other books. I fell asleep during my evening prayer and finally did not bother to pray at all. Before I realized it, I was a backslider. I had tasted sin and liked it. I decided I wanted more.

During this period, at the suggestion of my employer, I applied for the position of teacher at the one-room school in the mountains, where my husband had attended. Due to a lack of teachers, the school had been closed for four years. I intended to teach several years, save my money, then go to college and get my degree. The superintendent of schools for the county had known me since childhood and agreed to the proposal.

So I became a teacher. I boarded in the home of my future husband. Sad to say, I quickly laid aside any indications of being a Christian and threw morality to the winds. Before the second school year began, Gene and I were married.

Yes, I knew he drank. I was aware also of the history of alcohol use in his family. His father, who died the winter before I became a teacher, had operated a still during Prohibition.

Then why did I marry Gene?

First, I was woefully ignorant of the effects of alcohol. Gene and his younger brother, the only boys at home at the time, confined their drinking to times when they left the mountain and went to places where alcoholic beverages were available. This limited my contact with the product and its effects. Besides, I liked the romantic mood Gene assumed when drinking.

Although we had lived in the same house for nine months, Gene and I hardly knew each other. I marvel, as I look back, that our marriage survived. He may have loved me; he said he did. For my part, I am sure my emotions were more infatuation than love. You must know someone to love him, and I did not really know Gene.

Neither did I foresee the rocky road that lay ahead.

2. At Wit's End

No person taking his first drink expects to become an alcoholic, and Gene did not develop his addiction overnight. It happened gradually.

After our marriage we lived with my mother-in-law on the home place in a remote corner of Rockingham County, Virginia. I continued to teach in the one-room school. However, I soon discovered my marriage had been a dreadful mistake, but I was too stubborn and too proud to admit it.

No possibility existed for divorce. My parents had taught me divorce was wrong and "when you make your bed, you lie in it." Besides, neighbors on the mountain had said our marriage would last less than two months, and I was determined to prove them wrong.

Part of my unhappiness stemmed from my unrealistic expectation of marriage. I expected Gene to be a carbon copy of my father. My father drove to town for gas or groceries and returned promptly. Gene stood and talked for hours. He never came home when I thought he should.

Furthermore, my mother-in-law spoke of girls in the community who would willingly seduce her sons if given the opportunity. According to her, some of these individuals were not above creating those occasions! I found myself quickly becoming a very jealous wife.

No man enjoys coming home to an accusing, weeping wife. My inability to cope with the stress of marriage led to a deterioration in our already shaky relationship. After my mother-in-law accepted a job in the city, I was home alone almost every Sunday. I concluded from snapshots that appeared around the house that Gene and his younger brother, Orvil, were spending those Sundays with two young sirens who lived in the area. I did not know what, if anything, happened at those times, but I know I was very unhappy.

Conditions in our home improved when Orvil received his draft notice and left for the army. After that Gene stayed with me on Sundays. This change, however, did not solve the basic problems in our relationship. It merely delayed the crisis.

I cannot describe the effect Erma's arrival had on the family when she entered our home in October 1951. Gene's parents had desperately wanted a girl but had to settle for five boys. Although Gene's brothers (except for Edward, the oldest) married and had children, Erma remained the only granddaughter until the next generation.

Frequently the drinking bouts involving the brothers led to arguments that ended in physical blows. In spats of this nature, my mother-in-law always took the side of her youngest son, perhaps because Gene never defended himself. I wondered whether he felt that presenting his side of the disagreement would be useless.

One especially severe quarrel led to our decision to leave the mountain. Gene found a job as a farmhand with an employer who furnished housing and paid Gene a monthly wage. However, after six weeks this job proved unsatisfactory, and we moved to another farm about two miles from my home.

This farmer, Bob, appreciated Gene's skills in basic carpentry, vehicle maintenance and repair, and the ability to fix almost anything.

In spite of his skills, Gene's habit of drinking every other weekend cost him this job. Gene had worked for this farmer about one and a half years. Our first son, Leonard, was born during this period.

I did attend church sometimes while we lived on this

farm, but I did it only to soothe my conscience and to keep my parents happy. Although I realized that repentance and a renewed relationship with the Lord was the only solution to my troubled marriage, I feared that such a step could end my marriage. I was not ready to risk that yet.

When we left this location, we bought, with my father's help, a small place at the edge of Singer's Glen, Virginia. We moved there in December. Dennis was born into our family on March 9 of the following year. His arrival brought immediate conflict.

The Lord had given Erma and Leonard dark brown eyes like their father's. Gene's mother and all four of his brothers also had beautiful brown eyes. Not Dennis! He surveyed his world through mischievous, bright blue eyes. A mop of fuzzy blonde hair crowned his head.

My husband could not accept a Crider with blue eyes. I reasoned that if it was impossible for Gene to have a blue-eyed child, then it would also be impossible for me to have two brown-eyed ones!

That logic did not satisfy Gene. He decided that since Bob, our former employer, had blue eyes and blonde hair, I had "played around." Nothing I said changed that.

Turbulent years followed the move to the Glen. Due to his many abilities, Gene found work easily, but keeping a job proved to be a different story. First he worked for about eighteen months in a sawmill, helping saw logs into lumber. Then he spent a similar length of time in a bakery, where he twisted bread dough and placed it in pans to bake. Once he worked in a poultry operation that packaged pre-baked turkey with gravy. He also drove a truck that hauled poultry scraps from area processing plants to a rendering facility. For a time he worked in a mill that manufactured feed for the large chicken and turkey farms in Virginia. I never learned whether his drinking directly caused his dismissal from these positions, but no doubt it was a contributing factor.

By this time Gene's drinking was no longer confined to every other weekend. When Saturday arrived, he would be off to town, and I knew what to expect when he returned. Gene often stayed out until early Sunday morning. At these times I lay in bed, listening for the sound of his truck to come around the turn just outside our bedroom window. When a vehicle drove by instead of stopping, I cried. I worried about where Gene might be and why he did not come home.

Generally Gene drank every weekend. The only exception to this occurred when we traveled, either as a family or when accompanying my parents on out-of-state visits to relatives. Gene was an excellent driver when sober, and my parents enjoyed traveling with him.

Gene always behaved like a gentleman with my parents, and he always wore a hat. Mama liked that, but most of all she appreciated his courteous behavior. "I never have to be afraid he'll embarrass us," she confided on one occasion; and he did not—until many years later.

I was too ashamed to tell my parents about conditions at home, partly because I feared betraying my own spiritual poverty in exposing Gene's addiction.

One Saturday night Gene did not return home. On Sunday the hours dragged by, but no Gene. I became frantic. I checked with neighbors and friends, but no one could help. Finally, about dusk, Gene ambled in, cocky, drunk, and not the least bit sorry for the worry he had caused us.

Gene continued this pattern. About once a month he disappeared on Saturday afternoon and did not come home until Sunday evening. To this day I do not know where or how he used that time. Although he drank every weekend, he managed to remain sober during the week while working, but he could not handle a day off.

The Lord used the distress this created for me as a means of bringing me back to Himself. Our youngest son, Keith, was almost a year old when in May of 1960 I decided I had gone through enough. Gene clearly did not care about me, so why should I lose my soul over him? If my salvation cost my marriage, so be it. I did not have anything worth living for in my marriage anyway.

At the same time I realized that the only hope for our marriage lay in Christ. If I returned to the Lord, the possibility existed for Gene's salvation. It also offered hope for the children. I had abused Erma, taking out my frustration on her rather than on Gene. I understood what I was doing but seemed powerless to change my behavior.

So, after counting the cost carefully and recognizing that it would cost me everything,* I rededicated my life to Jesus Christ.

* "So likewise, whosoever he be of you that forsaketh not all that he hath, he cannot be my disciple" (Luke 14:33).

3. Feed Bag Crisis

My commitment to the Lord plunged our home into chaos. This happened because Gene and I were no longer traveling the same road. Our destinations and goals in life now differed. We ordered our lives by different moral codes. Daily I sought to please my Lord. Gene had no such concern. He preferred to leave God completely out of family affairs.

Because I had expected conflict to occur, it did not take me by surprise when it happened. Having grown up in a Christian home, I was aware of "Think not that I am come to send peace on earth: I came not to send peace, but a sword. For I am come to set a man at variance against his father, and the daughter against her mother, and the daughter in law against her mother in law. And a man's foes shall be they of his own household" (Matthew 10:34-36).

My former life produced many situations that demanded attention. I immediately set out to amend those misdeeds. In several instances I needed to make restitution. Gene could not understand the necessity of paying back. He reasoned that if he had done something and gotten away with it, why should he go back and tell that person about it? As far as he was concerned the requirements of a holy God was not sufficient motivation to make restitution.

For example, during Gene's employment at the feed mill, he regularly brought home in his lunch box printed feed bags. These sacks could be used just like material purchased from bolts in a fabric store. I transformed these bags into dresses for myself and Erma, shirts for Gene and the boys, curtains for the kitchen, pillowcases, and other items needed around the house.

Because my conscience sometimes twitched, however, I occasionally told Gene, "I wish you wouldn't bring so many of these bags." But the next day when he arrived with an unusual or attractive pattern, I was just as likely to ask, "Are there any more like this?" He, of course, obliged me by bringing some home.

I realized before getting right with the Lord that I would have to deal with this issue and that it would involve me in a heated argument. It did. If I had not encouraged Gene to steal those bags, I might have escaped responsibility for their presence in our home, but I doubt it. After all, I used them knowing where they came from, although Gene insisted that it was all right to take them.

After I contacted the feed mill about the sacks, two officers from the mill drove out to our home to collect the bags. But just a few days before the men's arrival, Gene took the remaining bags to the home of a friend to prevent their return to the company. When the mill sent us a bill for the sacks, Gene forbade me to pay it.

Although I understood the law of sowing and reaping, I failed to recognize at first how it applied to feed bags. I did not realize that since Gene had taken the sacks a just God would expect him to pay for them! Because I did not understand this, I assured my husband that the Lord would take care of the money, and Gene would have no cause to worry.

After some time the Lord opened my understanding, and I saw the problem through His eyes. He also supplied the grace to face the mounting tension caused by Gene's refusal to give up the bags or to pay for them.

I recall a confrontation one evening when Gene hurled cruel and cutting accusations at me—for hours, it seemed. However, I felt nothing in my heart toward him but an overwhelming love. I realized that Christian friends were praying for me.

When I awoke the next morning, the Lord brought wonderful reassurance to my heart. He placed in my mind the words of David: "When I awake, I am still with thee" (Psalm 139:18). That knowledge enabled me to face the day with joy and with the confidence that His presence would be with me.

The stalemate over the feed bags lasted for several weeks until my mother-in-law mailed the company a check for the sacks. I found it ironic that my assertion to Gene did become fact: Setting this matter straight did not cost him a cent.

Gene felt in this instance that I had stabbed him in the back, and I understood that. The Lord, however, had placed in my heart the compelling necessity to make this wrong right, and I had to obey. Gene's mother agreed with him. "I never saw anyone change like Virginia," she declared, "and it wasn't all for the good." In coping with this frustration, Gene drank even more.

I determined also to obey the Lord in another area. As a young girl I had been taught that 1 Corinthians 11:1-16 applies to our time. I knew the Lord desires Christian women to cover or veil their heads when they pray or engage in conversation of a spiritual nature (prophesying). But I had abandoned this practice when Gene and I were married.

Gene hated my veiling. One day while drunk he jerked the veil off my head and threw it into the smoldering fire in our living room stove. Later, when I opened the stove door to replenish the coal, there, in perfect form, lay the remains of my veil! The Lord spoke to me through that experience. "Stand your ground," He encouraged. "I am with you, Satan is not going to prevail. You'll come through the fire intact just as that veil has." I thanked God and replaced the ruined veiling with a white kerchief.

The biggest change that occurred in our marriage with my renewed commitment to the Lord took place in me. I no longer cried and begged Gene to stop drinking. Unlike some men who may find their wives' tears impossible to resist, tears provoked no sympathy from Gene. Instead, they angered him. I accepted the fact my husband was an alcoholic and determined to live my life, in spite of his addiction, to the glory of God.

Soon I discovered that living with an alcoholic in a God-honoring manner placed certain restrictions on me. It also brought many blessings.

4. You Have No Right

In finding my way during those early days of my walk with the Lord, I discovered several "rights" I had to lay aside.

No matter what Gene did or said to me, I had no right to be unkind or nasty to him. The Scripture enforcing this is Ephesians 4:32, "And be ye kind one to another, tenderhearted, forgiving one another, even as God for Christ's sake hath forgiven you."

This verse carries no qualifications such as "Be kind to others when they treat you nicely" or "Show kindness to others only if they show compassion to you." God's Word allows no loopholes for a sharp tongue. Many times I found myself apologizing for my sharp tongue after failing to control it.

I also learned I had no right to insist on my own way. The Crider family gathered for a reunion each September. I dreaded these meetings because of the use of alcohol, but my change of direction added another thorn, the location.

Previously the reunion had taken place at a popular resort with a public swimming pool adjacent to the picnic area. In another part of the resort, couples could be seen dancing to loud music. This atmosphere made me uncomfortable, and I wished to avoid it.

Surprisingly, as I look back, the thing that bothered me most about this setting was the immodesty of the men. I did not want to attend that reunion.

Gene misunderstood my reluctance. He accused, "You just don't want to see Eddie."

Before my rededication I had asked Edward, Gene's oldest brother, not to bring alcohol when he came to visit us. To Gene, and also to Edward, this amounted to saying, "Don't come." I did not realize this and was unaware of the rift my action created. Upon learning of it, I wrote to Edward and asked his forgiveness for what I had said. Never mind that our views on what had actually been said differed!

I protested to Gene that Edward had nothing to do with my hesitation to attend the reunion. I simply did not like the location. "Too good for the rest of the Criders, is that it?" Gene sneered.

"No, it isn't that," I assured him. One word led to another and suddenly, in his intoxicated state, Gene slapped me hard on the left cheek. As Jesus instructs (see Matthew 5:39) I turned the other cheek, and Gene also struck that one. Immediately he became contrite and began calling me "honey," something he never did when he was sober. He apologized profusely and begged me to go along to the reunion. In this case I saw no clear mandate from the Lord, no "Thou shalt not"; so I went. In other words, I submitted to my husband.

I also relinquished my "right" to grumble and complain, either about what I had to put up with or about what I had to do without.

Why is it wrong for a wife to complain when her husband comes home late? Or nag when he spends money for liquor that should have been used for food or shoes? Why must she accept injustice calmly?

I discovered that Titus 3:2, 3 commands us "to speak evil of no man"—husbands included! "For we ourselves also were sometimes foolish, disobedient [ouch!], deceived, serving divers lusts and pleasures, living in malice and envy, hateful, and hating one another." Most of those things described me outside of Christ. That being the case, I had no right to speak evil of someone else, especially my husband.

Bitterness had to go. I could no longer chastise

Gene—aloud or in my thoughts—for not meeting my expectations. I dared not harbor resentment toward him because his negligence forced me to cancel my plans. I must silence the voice that whispered, "Yes, if Gene didn't spend so much for alcohol, I wouldn't need to skimp on groceries!" Hebrews 12:15 warns, "Looking diligently lest any man fail of the grace of God; lest any root of bitterness springing up trouble you, and thereby many be defiled." When we allow bitterness to creep in, we are not availing ourselves of the grace of God.

Accepting my husband's alcoholism meant I had to decide to live within the boundaries his addiction imposed. I could not expect a full closet of beautiful clothing. My pantry shelves would lack items considered essential by many cooks. Fortunately, I had grown up in a poor home during the Depression and was not accustomed to luxuries, so my lifestyle changed little.

I learned also I had no right to expect justice from my husband. A person operating under the influence of alcohol is incapable of justice. Therefore, I came to accept the fact that deceit and lies become the norm rather than truth and right. "Resist not evil" (Matthew 5:39) to me meant, "Don't fight against the injustice and unfairness. Learn to live with it. Leave vengeance to God."

One of the hardest rights for me to lay aside was to expect consideration and understanding. Every woman desires to be understood by her husband. She relishes his consideration and wants to be appreciated. I finally recognized I might just as well forget these cherished rights. As an alcoholic, Gene did not have the inner qualities required for such expressions.

Faced with all these negatives, how can the wife of an alcoholic possibly hope to live a happy, productive life?

5. Security—Where Do I Find It?

Can the wife of an alcoholic know happiness while coping with the abuse, lies, and indignities accompanying his addiction? What elements need to be present for her to experience joy while living with constant turmoil, pain, and trouble?

Common sense suggests that in a home filled with confusion, the qualities that bring joy must come from outside that home. The only solution to the heartache and misery accompanying life with an alcoholic lies, not in things, but in a person, and that person is Jesus Christ.

Why does the presence of Christ alter the situation? Why does allegiance to Him make a difference? Perhaps some examples from my experience will clarify this.

Before receiving Christ in my heart as Lord and Saviour, I suffered from a deep sense of guilt and fear. I dreaded going on the highway with Gene because of the possibility of an accident. Riding with an alcoholic at the wheel of a vehicle is scary! I knew what my destiny would be, should I die.

Turning to Christ with all my heart removed the fear and guilt of my sin. Peace flooded my soul and joy entered my heart. I remember especially the fragrance of the locust blossoms that spring. Those trees had stood in our fields for years, but not until May of 1960 did their aroma penetrate my awareness.

I looked at life from a new perspective. As Paul states in 2 Corinthians 5:17, "Therefore if any man be in Christ, he is a new creature: old things are passed away; behold, all things are become new."

Along with the new outlook on life because of salvation in Jesus came new security. I never felt secure, cared for, and protected with Gene. Not knowing where he was or how he was spending his hours away from home left me in a state of constant instability.

Christ changed that. I no longer sought security in a husband upon whom I could not depend and of whose love I could not be certain. I found my security in One who promised never to leave me or forsake me (Hebrews 13:5) and who always keeps His promises. I know He loves me because He *died* for me.

Not only does Jesus love me, but also He has at His disposal all the power in the universe. He claims as His "every beast of the forest" and the "cattle upon a thousand hills." He says, "The world is mine, and the fulness thereof" (Psalm 50:10, 12).

This great God who owns and controls the universe, who numbers the stars and calls each one by name, says, "Call upon me in the day of trouble: I will deliver thee, and thou shalt glorify me" (Psalm 50:15).

The invitation to bring my trouble to Christ seemed sensible to me. Since everything in the universe belongs to Him, surely He could channel those resources into my hands in response to my call. In the years that have followed this decision to trust Christ, He has never failed me, although many times I fall short of His glory.

Gene lost his job about the same time I returned to the Lord. During this time the children were exposed to mumps at school. Since Gene had not had them as a child, he also came down with the disease.

With no money coming in due to Gene's illness, we soon found our pantry and refrigerator shelves empty. The Lord, however, provided a huge box of groceries from an unidentified source. I still do not know whom the Lord used to supply our need, but it must have been someone with a large family. As my father said, "Who else would think to purchase applesauce in gallon-size cans?"

Jesus brought security and stability in another area. Gene found what was supposed to be a temporary job with the Virginia Department of Highways. He worked with a survey crew who drilled core samples to discover the type of soil beneath the right-of-way where new roads were to be built. This group of men also determined how much and what kinds of rock lay under the surface, the amount of soil to be moved, and many other things. Gene enjoyed this work.

When the surveying was completed, the state personnel decided they could use Gene on the bridge gang. This crew was responsible for maintaining the bridges in the county.

The work of the bridge gang consisted mostly of painting the metal spans already in existence. These men applied a rustproof finish to the upper and lower parts of the metal bridge. The crew rigged a mobile scaffolding beneath the floor of the bridge. They sat on this structure while painting the underside of the span and moved it as the work progressed. Because they often worked high above water, the men had to be unafraid of heights. Occasionally a man "froze" under the bridge and had to be forcibly removed. Gene, however, scrambled over and under the bridges without fear.

Somehow the state discovered Gene's mechanical ability, and someone told his supervisor, "Gene is too good with machinery to keep him on the bridge gang." So Gene graduated to the road crew. He began by operating the sheep-foot (packer) and roller. Soon he moved up to using a front-end loader and a bulldozer. Finally he worked with the large motorized pans that moved huge amounts of soil from one spot to another.

The state learned also of Gene's knowledge of welding. His supervisor sent him to school to refine his skill in this art. Later Gene attended, again at state expense, another school where he studied the procedure for using dynamite. However, working with dynamite gave him headaches, and he avoided it when possible.

After Gene had been with the highway department for one year, his employer shifted him from the hourly wage scale to a salary basis. Gene remained with the state until he retired, a period of twenty-six years. I doubt whether Gene gave any credit to the Lord for his lengthy employment with the state, but I do.

Satan tested the reality of Christ as my security. During the days of conflict over the feed bags, Gene informed me several times that he was going to pack up and leave. Since I no longer looked to him for my security, I did not try to stop him.

A more compelling reason existed, however, for allowing him to go if he so chose. Why would I tell my husband whom I loved that he was free to leave?

Paul counsels the believing wife of an unsaved husband: "And the woman which hath an husband that believeth not, and if he be pleased to dwell with her, let her not leave him. For the unbelieving husband is sanctified by the wife, . . . But if the unbelieving depart, *let him depart*" (1 Corinthians 7:13-15). Though I dared not walk out on Gene, I must be willing to let him go.

Had I begged and pleaded with Gene to stay, he immediately would have listed the conditions to which I must agree if I wished him to remain. Those stipulations would surely have hobbled my efforts to live a victorious Christian life. I thank God that because of my knowledge of His Word I escaped that trap.

Gene did not leave. I believe he used the threat to try to gain leverage and force me to alter my stand for Christ. Since Christ had become my security, I could freely open my hand and say, "If you want to go, the door is open. I won't try to stop you."

For the sake of the children, a friend of mine separated from her alcoholic husband. However, she obeyed the instruction of 1 Corinthians 7:11: "But and if she depart, let her remain unmarried, or be reconciled to her husband."

God used the crisis caused by this separation to help the husband clearly see the seriousness of his wrong living, and he accepted Christ. Along with his redemption came the restoration of the family.

The Lord deals with each of us according to our individual personalities and needs. Before a wife takes such a drastic step as separation from her mate, she must be sure the voice she is listening to is that of the Holy Spirit and not her own wishful thinking! Godly counsel is also critical.

Being secure in Christ frees the energy formerly consumed by worry and fear to be channeled into constructive activities.

Nevertheless, I discovered absolutes that must accompany my walk with the Lord and that are essential to my security in living with my alcoholic husband. I'll define some of these absolutes and their roles in the following chapters.

6. The Absolute Word

What are absolutes? Why do we need them? How do absolutes fit into living with an alcoholic?

Do you remember the kidnapping of Patricia Hearst some years ago? The results of her abuse and confinement led her to eventually abandon the training of her youth and join her kidnappers in robbing a bank.

In contrast to the experience of Miss Hearst, I have on my bookshelf an account written by Claude Fly, an American who worked for the United Nations Food and Agricultural Organization in Montevideo, Uruguay. A group of Tupamaros, part of an underground terrorist organization, captured him and held him prisoner for seven months. He spent much of this time in a wire cage hidden behind a heavy curtain in a damp, cold basement. His captors allowed him out of the cage only to see to his personal needs.

How did this man maintain his sanity under such conditions? He asked for and received a Bible. He devoured it, searching for and finding answers to his dilemma. The influence of this Book enabled him to pray for his kidnappers and brought about his deliverance.

The experiences of these two persons illustrate the necessity for an absolute. Patty Hearst lacked that influence in her life, and she caved in to circumstances. Claude Fly possessed an anchor that enabled him to triumph over his confinement.

An absolute describes something that is rock solid, firm, immovable. It stands untouched by the effects of time and the attacks of Satan. An absolute remains strong even when everything around it seems to be crumbling.

Why do we need an absolute? With the turmoil and confusion surrounding us, we must have a rock, a "nail in a sure place" (Isaiah 22:23), on which to anchor our faith. As Isaiah so beautifully states, we must have a "hiding place from the wind, and a covert from the tempest; as rivers of water in a dry place, as the shadow of a great rock in a weary land" (Isaiah 32:2).

Where is that "hiding place from the wind," that "shadow of a great rock in a weary land"? Where do I find that "covert from the tempest" and the "rivers of water in a dry place"? In other words, how do I recognize an absolute, something that stands firm while the tempest rages?

The psalmist says, "For ever, O LORD, thy word is settled in heaven" (Psalm 119:89). He tells us the Word of God will never change. It is established, fixed. It stands forever. It is absolute.

What does that have to do with me? Unless I am convinced that the Bible is absolute, that it is the inspired Word of God, I will be unprepared to stake my life and my future on it. Because successfully coping with the problems related to alcoholism demands obedience to the Word, I must be certain of the origin of this Book. I must acknowledge its authority to instruct and to correct me.

The constant disturbances in my home demanded answers. How could I handle the accusations and the lies Gene hurled at me? What could I do about his lack of consideration? Would I have to put up with his verbal abuse? How could I cope with the injury and insult?

I knew the Word of God contained the answers to those questions, and I set out to find them. I recalled how I came to be in my current straits—through my neglect of the Scripture—and I determined to be faithful in reading and obeying God's Word.

Even though the Lord knows our needs before we ask,

He wants us to bring our requests to Him. He wants us to acknowledge our poverty and inability to help ourselves as He invites, "Call unto me, and I will answer thee, and shew thee great and mighty things, which thou knowest not" (Jeremiah 33:3).

The Lord will not show us these "great and mighty things," however, unless we call on Him. Once we have asked, where do we look for the answers? To hear from God we must turn to His Word.

The Lord does not always reveal the solutions to our problems immediately. Sometimes He allows us to search for them. Sometimes He may test us to see whether we really want the answer.

In Proverbs 2:3-5 Solomon counsels, "Yea, if thou criest after knowledge, and liftest up thy voice for understanding; if thou seekest her as silver, and searchest for her as for hid treasures; *then* [emphasis mine] shalt thou understand the fear of the LORD, and find the knowledge of God."

Notice the verbs Solomon used to describe how we are to go about looking for wisdom. We *cry* after it; we *lift up* our voices. We *search* for it as we would for silver or gold. We expend great energy in seeking to make a good living for our families. If we wish to acquire understanding and knowledge, Solomon says we must seek for it diligently as one searches for riches.

Although we may not discover the answer to our difficulty at once, reading the Word of God offers other benefits. Just as food and water are required to sustain life, spiritual nourishment is essential for maintaining life in Christ. Searching the Scriptures nurtures the soul with the bread and water of life. Reading the Word is even more necessary to our spiritual well-being than food is to our bodies. The physical body dies, but the soul exists forever.

I established a daily Bible reading schedule that

enabled me to read the Book from cover to cover in one year. I found this to be so beneficial that I still read the Bible through annually. Even if you do not read your Bible through yearly as I do, you must develop a daily reading program if you want to live victoriously.

The Lord supplies guidance and direction through His Word. I discovered that I needed to go back and make more wrongs right. Considering the hassle over the feed sacks, it would have been much easier to make further restitution without Gene's knowledge. The Lord prompted, however, "Provide things honest in the sight of all men" (Romans 12:17), and that included my husband. He must have the privilege of reading the letters I wrote. Even if he did not avail himself of that opportunity, it had to be open to him.

Some of the persons who received my letters of apology later told Gene about them. Had he been unaware of them when his friends mentioned them, it would have been a shock to him. He probably would have felt I had stabbed him in the back once again.

Through numerous personal encounters, the Lord taught me the truth of Proverbs 15:1: "A soft answer turneth away wrath: but grievous words stir up anger." This principle stands true after many testings: A gentle answer nips a quarrel in the bud before it can develop, but complaining words lead directly to conflict.

In addition to guidance and direction, the Word of God provides hope and comfort. Passages such as Psalm 37 brought solace to my heart. David tells us not to fret about the evildoer but to "trust in the LORD" (verse 3). Furthermore, we are to "delight" in Him (verse 4). If we do this, He will give us the desires of our hearts. This doesn't mean that God does for us whatever we want. But He certainly did grant one of my deep desires when Gene stopped drinking in August 1976.

In Psalm 37:6, David says the Lord will "bring forth

thy righteousness as the light, and thy judgment as the noonday." He will take care of the accusations and lies; we need not worry about them.

I especially like Psalm 37:7: "Rest in the LORD, and wait patiently for him." How do I "rest in the Lord"? I do so by believing His promises and by trusting Him to follow through on His Word. When He says in Romans 8:28 "that all things work together for good to them that love God," I accept that as truth and expect to see His hand bring good out of seemingly impossible situations.

Resting in the Lord means that I recognize His hand at work in the everyday happenings of my life.

For example, one day I spoke to a friend about something I found unusually difficult to accept. I do not recall what had occurred. My friend reasoned, "Virginia, look at it this way, if Gene isn't kicking up his heels, you know nothing is bothering him. When he bucks and kicks, we know the Holy Spirit is at work and that Gene is resisting His probing."

How true! If I prayed for Gene's salvation and expected the Lord to answer, then I must also expect to see a reaction to the convicting power of the Holy Spirit. My friend's counsel helped me through many difficult times.

Another passage that yielded comfort during troubled times is 1 Peter 3:15, 16: "But sanctify the Lord God in your hearts: and be ready always to give an answer to every man that asketh you a reason of the hope that is in you with meekness and fear: having a good conscience; that, whereas they speak evil of you, as of evildoers, they may be ashamed that falsely accuse your good conversation in Christ."

How many times Gene mistook my intentions and accused me of evil motives! Peter gave me hope. "Sanctify the Lord God in your hearts," he counseled. In other words, Set Christ in your heart as Lord.

Installing Christ in my heart as Lord meant that my allegiance belonged to Him. I was accountable to Him. As long as my life pleased the Lord, how Gene felt about it was of secondary importance. After all, I will not stand before Gene on the day of judgment. I will face my Lord.

Peter further warns us to be prepared at all times to explain our actions from the Word of God. We should be able to Scripturally justify why we make restitution, write a letter, or place a controversial phone call.

If we follow his directions, Peter declares, the time will come when our husbands will be ashamed of the false charges they have laid against us. We need to remember that. This promise should bring cheer to our hearts.

The Word of God allows no disobedience from us. Perhaps the hardest area for me to work through was anger.

Before my recommitment to Christ, I allowed anger to control my mind. In searching the Scriptures, I soon realized that I would have to deal with my anger. Several verses convicted me: "But now ye also put off all these; anger, wrath, malice" (Colossians 3:8); "For the wrath of man worketh not the righteousness of God" (James 1:20); "Cease from anger, and forsake wrath: fret not thyself in any wise to do evil" (Psalm 37:8).

When I stopped to analyze my anger and the results it produced, I realized the truth of James's words. Usually my bouts of anger sprang from an injured ego or trampled pride. In considering the cause of my anger, I had to conclude that it did not bring about the righteous life God desired for me. Anger had to be weeded out.

A Book of absolute truth requires unconditional faith and obedience. However, this same Book contains absolute promises of unmeasurable value for those who love and obey it. The Bible holds the key to joy and victory for the wife of an alcoholic.

The next chapter is on prayer.

7. Pray—Without Ceasing

We have discussed the Word of God and the role it must fill for the wife of an alcoholic. We affirmed that the Word must be obeyed if the wife is to live a happy and productive life. God has provided another instrument to help the alcoholic's wife cope with her circumstances.

Effective communication flows between those communicating. As God speaks to us through His Word, we need to respond to Him through prayer.

God encourages us to approach His throne in prayer: "Call upon me, and I will answer" (Psalm 91:15). He wants us to draw near to Him. James assures us, "Draw nigh to God, and he will draw nigh to you" (James 4:8).

Jesus attaches important conditions to prayer that cover every area of living. He says, "If ye abide in me, and my words abide in you, ye shall ask what ye will, and it shall be done unto you" (John 15:7). His words must live in us, and we must live in Him (Galatians 2:20). To amplify, Jesus says simply, "You have to know my teaching, and you have to obey it. If you do this, you can ask anything you wish of Me and receive it."

With this background, let us talk about prayer. Why do we need to pray? Perhaps the most compelling reason for prayer stems from the fact that we stand in such great need. Through prayer we avail ourselves of the unlimited grace of God and His boundless riches, whether temporal or spiritual.

David expresses my attitude toward prayer in Psalm 40:16, 17: "Let all those that seek thee rejoice and be glad in thee. . . . But I am poor and needy; yet the Lord thinketh upon me." Yes, I am poor and I am needy, but the Lord can supply my deficiency through prayer.

The Book of Psalms records other prayers of David: "I sought the LORD, and he heard me. . . . This poor man cried, and the LORD heard him, and saved him out of all his troubles" (Psalm 34:4, 6). These words echo the sentiment of my heart.

I can also identify with David when he said, "Oh that I had wings like a dove! for then would I fly away, and be at rest" (Psalm 55:6). But what balm soothed my mind when I remembered that Jesus invites, "Come unto me, . . . I will give you rest" (Matthew 11:28)! I did not have to escape to the desert to find rest. All I needed to do was come to Jesus in prayer.

Why is prayer necessary? What other means can I use to deal with the anger that threatens to overwhelm me when my alcoholic husband upsets a cherished holiday by failing to come home? How else do I cope with his tirade against how much I spend for groceries, especially after I have trimmed my spending to the minimum? To whom can I turn when he forbids me to attend prayer meetings or the Sunday evening services? I can always go to the Lord, and He brings peace, hope, and comfort as I seek His face through the Word and through prayer. The Word and prayer belong together; they complement each other.

James encourages us to pray for wisdom. I discovered that I needed much wisdom in meeting daily challenges. "If any of you lack wisdom, let him ask of God, that giveth to all men liberally, and upbraideth not; and it shall be given him" (James 1:5). Did you catch it? Wisdom will be given to those who ask for it. The beautiful aspect of this promise is that the Lord does not scold us because we lack wisdom. He knows our poverty and invites us to tap into His wealth. How wonderful!

James also asks, "Is any among you afflicted [distressed]? let him pray" (James 5:13). Who among wives of alcoholics has not been in distress? James tells us to pray, to bring our troubles to our Father who loves us.

Peter adds that to humble ourselves before God results in "Casting all [our] care upon him; for he careth for [us]" (1 Peter 5:7).

James also offers this counsel: "Resist the devil, and he will flee from you" (James 4:7). How do we stand against Satan, the enemy of our souls? We use the power of prayer, coupled with the Word of God.

When should we pray? Most of us probably think of prayer as a formal exercise, of kneeling beside our beds and talking with the Lord. Jesus tells us to enter our closets and shut the door when we pray. Because of the layout of our house, I found "entering a closet" impossible. I solved the problem by using a small outdoor building as a place of prayer.

Another solution eventually presented itself. I learned to pray "on the run." When I first began praying silently in my mind as I worked about the house, I wondered, *Does the Lord accept this kind of prayer?* The Lord reassured me through Psalm 139:2: "Thou understandest my thought afar off." I reasoned too that since the Holy Spirit inhabited my body, He surely could discern my thoughts.

I learned to pray in good times as well as in times that try the soul. In spite of the heartache alcoholism brings to the home, we can always find reasons to be thankful. How we need to thank God for His goodness.

I thanked God for the weekdays—Monday through Friday—when Gene usually remained sober. I praised God also for the commendable traits Gene possessed. He was a good worker and he provided for us. When sober, he displayed a pleasant, likeable personality, and neighbors loved him. When Gene was not drinking he usually treated us well. Sometimes we become so wrapped up in the negatives of living with an alcoholic that we forget to be thankful.

How do I pray? I continue "instant in prayer" (Romans 12:12). I also "pray without ceasing" (1 Thessalonians 5:17). That means I do not give up, but I follow Jesus' admonition to "pray, and not to faint" (Luke 18:1).

I must pray in faith. Jesus said, "What things soever ye desire, when ye pray, believe that ye receive them, and ye shall have them" (Mark 11:24). James says I must ask, "nothing wavering" (James 1:6). That means I do not doubt the Lord's promise to hear and to answer my plea.

John adds a qualification to our prayers. We must ask according to the will of God, if we are to pray effectively. "And this is the confidence that we have in him, that, if we ask any thing according to his will, he heareth us. And if we know that he hear us, whatsoever we ask, we know that we have the petitions that we desired of him" (1 John 5:14, 15).

How can I pray "in the will of God" for my alcoholic husband? I may intercede for his salvation since I know it is not the will of God "that any should perish, but that all should come to repentance" (2 Peter 3:9).

We know the Word of God condemns drunkenness. This is another good reason to pray for an alcoholic. I wish I did not have to quote these references, but the Word of God tells us drunkenness will keep a person from inheriting the kingdom of God. Galatians 5:19-21 states: "Now the works of the flesh are manifest, which are these; . . . drunkenness, . . . they which do such things shall not inherit the kingdom of God."

This message is repeated in 1 Corinthians 6:9, 10: "Know ye not that the unrighteous shall not inherit the kingdom of God? Be not deceived: . . . drunkards . . . shall [not] inherit the kingdom of God."

Although I recognized that Gene's primary need was the new birth, I also felt free—in light of the seriousness of alcohol addiction—to ask the Lord for Gene's deliverance from that habit.

In Philippians 4:6, we are told to pray rather than worry. "Be careful for nothing; but in every thing by prayer and supplication with thanksgiving let your requests be made known unto God." This verse allows me the freedom to pray about anything and everything, from a misplaced sock to providing us with a better car and funds to pay the electric bill.

Jesus tells us specifically in Luke 6:28, "Bless them that curse you, and pray for them which despitefully use you." Surely this applies to the alcoholic! Many times I felt "despitefully used" by Gene. I recall sitting in the living room one Sunday evening and hearing Gene in the kitchen berating "the old woman" (me) to his mother, who seemed to be listening with willing ears.

The Lord Jesus commands us to pray for those who mistreat us. I believe this directive enables us to forgive. We cannot pray earnestly for someone and at the same time hold a grudge against him.

Peter enlarges on this theme. He cites the example of Jesus in dealing with injustice. Although Peter specifically addresses servants, the principle applies also to us.

"Servants, be subject to your masters . . . not only to the good and gentle, but also to the froward [perverse]. For this is thankworthy, if a man for conscience toward God endure grief, suffering wrongfully. For what glory is it, if, when ye be buffeted for your faults, ye shall take it patiently? but if, when ye do well, and suffer for it, ye take it patiently, this is acceptable with God. For even hereunto were ye called: because Christ also suffered for us, leaving us an example, that ye should follow his steps: . . . Who, when he was reviled, reviled not again; when he suffered, he threatened not; but committed himself to him that judgeth righteously: Who his own self bare our sins in his own body on the tree" (1 Peter

2:18-24).

Christ, Peter informs us, is our example in unjust suffering. Christ demonstrated by His own life how to handle physical abuse. Jesus did not verbally threaten those who misused Him. Instead, He committed Himself to the Father who always judges rightly.

We are to follow Jesus' example. We are not to retaliate or threaten when we endure abuse. Rather, as Jesus did, we are to pray for those who are treating us unjustly.

I discovered that Scripture often expresses the desire of my heart better than I can. I frequently used David's words when burdens became heavy. "Make haste, O God, to deliver me; make haste to help me, O LORD. Let them be ashamed and confounded that seek after my soul: let them be turned backward, . . . that desire my hurt. . . . Let all those that seek thee rejoice and be glad in thee: and let such as love thy salvation say continually, Let God be magnified. But I am poor and needy: make haste unto me, O God: thou art my help and my deliverer; O LORD, make no tarrying" (Psalm 70:1-5). Doesn't that echo the cry of your heart? It did mine.

I love Isaiah 64:1-5 also: "Oh that thou wouldest rend the heavens, that thou wouldest come down, that the mountains might flow down at thy presence, as when the melting fire burneth, the fire causeth the water to boil, to make thy name known to thine adversaries, that the nations may tremble at thy presence! When thou didst terrible things which we looked not for, thou camest down, the mountains flowed down at thy presence. For since the beginning of the world men have not heard, nor perceived by the ear, neither hath the eye seen, O God, beside thee, what he hath prepared for him that waiteth for him. Thou meetest him that rejoiceth and worketh righteousness, those that remember thee in thy ways."

I am not sure why this passage appealed to me so strongly. Perhaps I felt my situation was desperate enough that it merited the Lord's "rending the heavens" to come to my assistance. However that may have been, the assurance that the Lord meets the person who rejoices, who works righteousness, and who remembers Him in His ways always comforted me and still does. And perhaps, since Isaiah had the boldness to utter this prayer for Israel, it would be permissible for me to use it for my family.

The Lord treasures our prayers. In the Book of Revelation John describes a scene in heaven where the four living creatures and the twenty-four elders all have harps and golden bowls full of incense, which are the prayers of the saints. John reveals more about this subject in Revelation 8:3-5: "And another angel came and stood at the altar, . . . and there was given unto him much incense, that he should offer it with the prayers of all saints upon the golden altar which was before the throne. And the smoke of the incense, which came with the prayers of the saints, ascended up before God out of the angel's hand. And the angel took the censer, and filled it with fire of the altar, and cast it into the earth: and there were voices, and thunderings, and lightnings, and an earthquake."

Notice what took place on earth when the prayers of the saints ascended before God—thunder, lightning, and an earthquake. David gives a similar description in Psalm 18:6-9: "In my distress I called upon the LORD, . . . he heard my voice out of his temple, and my cry came before him, even into his ears. *Then* [emphasis mine] the earth shook and trembled; the foundations also of the hills moved and were shaken [an earthquake?]. . . . He bowed the heavens also, and came down."

Many times we find ourselves unable to express our concerns. We are unable to put our feelings into words.

In such times we want to remember the role of the Holy Spirit. "The Spirit itself maketh intercession for us with groanings which cannot be uttered" (Romans 8:26).

I cannot say that I ever sensed the earth shake in response to my prayers, but I do know the Lord heard and answered. Those answers were not always what I expected and did not always come at the time I had hoped they would, but in His wisdom the Lord replied in the way He knew would be best.

In a sense the Lord did rend the heavens and come down. Praise His name!

8. Fellowship

What is fellowship? I find it difficult to define. The best I can come up with follows:

Fellowship is the bond of love that exists between believers because of their mutual love for Christ and the empathy resulting from that bond. This definition, however, cannot convey the warmth, the caring, and the intense interaction of fellowship which exists between Christians.

What does fellowship have to do with the wife of the alcoholic? A newborn baby must have milk to grow, but no less important to its survival is tender loving care (TLC). Fellowship for the wife of the alcoholic compares to TLC for a baby. Both include the love, the warmth, and the caring that each person desperately needs. We usually find fellowship in a church.

Finding a church that believes the Word of God and teaches it may not be easy, but we dare not settle for less. Unless the members of the congregation accept the Bible as God's Holy Word, and unless they express this conviction in everyday living, the understanding and the warmth that the wife of the alcoholic must have for her survival will be lacking. Her spiritual well-being depends in a large degree on the support of a praying, loving, and caring congregation.

My small congregation holds Wednesday night prayer services. I never felt comfortable sharing my problems before the larger assembly; but in the intimacy of the prayer meeting I could express my concerns, knowing I would be understood and supported.

I recall an incident that took place in 1975. After we brought my mother-in-law to live with us, her sons decided a bathroom should be installed for her convenience. Since we received no financial compensation for caring for Granny, Gene's brothers agreed that she should pay for the installation of the bathroom. A carpenter brother from my church agreed to do the necessary remodeling.

One week Gene determined that he would stay at home and help. This would have been fine had he remained sober, but he drank all week. During this time my carpenter brother witnessed firsthand the devastation alcohol brought into our home.

Although the brother from church did not observe this incident, I will relate it as an example of the pressure I experienced during that week. Gene decided early in the week to purchase the bathroom fixtures. Because only I could sign the checks drawn on the temporary account set up to pay construction expenses, I had to accompany him.

When we arrived at the hardware store, Gene immediately began searching for his friend Joe, a salesman. Another clerk approached us and offered to assist us.

"No," Gene declared, "I have to see Joe."

"Joe isn't working today," the salesman told us.

"But I have to see Joe," Gene insisted belligerently.

"But Joe isn't working today," the clerk answered courteously. "May I help you?"

"But I have to see Joe," Gene declared. "He's going to get the bathtub for me at cost in his name. He told me he would."

The clerk looked at me. He turned back to Gene and said, "Joe isn't supposed to do that. It's against the rules."

When Gene finally realized that Joe was not to be found, he tried to strike a similar deal with this salesman. He, however, seemed unwilling to cooperate with Gene. I wanted nothing to do with this shady scheme, but what could I do?

After some thought, I decided to take a stand for right, even if Gene resented it. I encouraged the young man not to go against the rules. "Don't do anything you aren't supposed to," I cautioned. I know it sounds trite, but I felt I had to be on record as opposed to dishonesty. I wanted this young man to know that I had no part in the plot conceived by Gene and Joe.

We paid the full price for the bathtub and other bathroom fixtures.

By Wednesday evening my spiritual, mental, and physical resources were exhausted. When I asked for prayer that evening, my carpenter brother from church said, "I've been working there this week; I know what she is talking about."

I cried that entire evening. It felt so good to be cared for and understood. With this group I could relax, unwind, and not worry about appearances.

I know a woman whose alcoholic husband does not permit her to attend church on Sunday mornings. However, he does permit her to go to the midweek prayer services. Although this limited contact does not completely satisfy the woman's desire for fellowship, she thanks God for it.

The Sunday morning service fills another requirement for me. Although I read my Bible daily and pray constantly, I still need to sit in the Sunday school class, take part in the discussion, and hear the Word of God preached. While this meets my need for fellowship, it also stimulates and challenges my thinking.

A Sunday morning discussion returns to my mind. The lesson centered around a confrontation Jesus had with the Pharisees about eating without first washing one's hands (Mark 7:1-20). Jesus responded to their complaints by saying that it is not what enters a person that makes him unclean but what comes out of him that defiles him.

How can that be? I wondered to myself.

I thought of what whiskey and beer did to Gene when they entered his body. Gene sometimes used language during those times that he never used when sober—foul words that most people do not utter in decent company. Didn't whiskey and beer do that to him? Didn't they defile him?

When I stopped to consider this dilemma, the Lord showed me that the sin already present in Gene's heart defiled him. Alcohol merely liberated and intensified its effects.

That incident illustrates what church attendance can do for us. If we actively participate in the service, it stimulates our minds. Stimulation produces growth, and without growth we become stagnant. But we must "turn ourselves on" and "tune in" to what is being presented. We cannot expect the teacher or pastor to do it for us!

I remember another Sunday morning when Leonard, our oldest son, was about twelve years old. Leonard hated to change clothes, and this particular morning he dallied more than usual in getting his shoes on. I tried to hurry the process.

"Buckshot [Gene's nickname for Leonard], you don't have to go to church if you don't want to," Gene said. He stabbed me with a glare, daring me to challenge him. I knew better than to do that, so I waited for our son's decision.

Leonard did not go to church that Sunday.

Can you imagine the thought that raced through my mind as I drove to church with my three children? How would I handle this situation? I must respect my husband's authority as the head of the home, but I could not allow Leonard to use this event as an opportunity to stop attending church. Might he, I wondered, attempt the "Dad-says-I-don't-have-to-go" ploy? What *could* I do?

The song leader that morning chose to lead that marvelous old hymn, "How Firm a Foundation." I am sure I had sung it many times before, but the words never penetrated my mind as they did that day. I do not know of another hymn that would have fit my situation better.

How firm a foundation, ye saints of the Lord,
Is laid for your faith in His excellent Word!
What more can He say than to you He hath said,
Who unto the Saviour for refuge have fled?

Fear not, I am with thee, oh, be not dismayed;
For I am thy God, and will still give thee aid;
I'll strengthen thee, help thee, and cause thee to stand,
Upheld by My righteous, omnipotent hand.

When through the deep waters I cause thee to go,
The rivers of sorrow shall not overflow.
For I will be with thee thy troubles to bless,
And sanctify to thee thy deepest distress.

When through fiery trials thy pathway shall lie,
My grace, all sufficient, shall be thy supply;
The flame shall not hurt thee, I only design
Thy dross to consume and thy gold to refine.

The soul that on Jesus hath leaned for repose
I will not, I will not desert to his foes;
That soul, though all hell should endeavor to shake,
I'll never, no, never, no, never forsake.

—George Keith, 1787

Can you understand how the Lord used that magnificent hymn to speak to my troubled mind? He would not forsake me, nor would He allow Satan the victory! Furthermore, He would "sanctify to me" the distress of this day and use it to honor Himself. But I had to be in church that Sunday for the Lord to supply His healing balm through that song.

The wife of the alcoholic needs another form of fellowship. Some things cannot be spoken of, even in the closely knit group of believers like a prayer group. She must have a confidante, preferably a Christian woman who is mature, someone who walks with the Lord, whom she can trust not to talk to others and who will pray with her and for her. If you ask, the Lord can lead you to such a person.

I recall Memorial Day 1970. Something occurred then that I have shared with only one person besides Erma and my special friend, Catherine. This event disturbed me tremendously. Although I visited my pastor and asked him to pray, I could not bring myself to explain to him what had happened. You too may face such a crisis and need a confidante.

There will be times also when you will want someone to rejoice with you—times when sharing with a larger circle or the wider church family would not be appropriate. Here again you must have a friend whom you can trust.

In addition to Catherine, I also confided in another friend, a younger woman who lived in a distant state. I found Lois to be a sympathetic "pop-off" valve, one who was always ready to listen and a friend on whom I could rely.

Not only could I depend on Lois to listen (through my letters), but I could also be sure she would warn me if my attitudes or actions deviated from the Word of God. That is what true friendship is all about!

Lois saved my letters down through the years. In 1989 she returned to me those she had accumulated during our years of correspondence. Those letters proved very useful to me in reconstructing the account of our son's rebellion in Chapter 11.

In emphasizing the necessity for a sister-friend, I do

not want to leave the impression that we should not share with our pastors. Our pastors care about our problems and need to know, but some things are more suitably shared among women—perhaps the pastor's wife. In addition, if we women communicate among ourselves, our husbands have no grounds for accusing us of running to the preacher every time something goes wrong!

I thank God for the fellowship of believers at my small church. I want to publicly thank them for standing behind me for the past thirty years.

May the Lord bless you, Morning View!

9. Submission—A Joy

How do I live with my alcoholic husband? Does the Word of God offer further guidelines? If so, what are those directives and where do I find them?

The command of the Lord I think comes perhaps hardest to the wife of the alcoholic is that she "reverence" her husband (Ephesians 5:33). What does that mean? How can she do it? Why does she need to reverence her husband?

Another translation says we should respect our husbands. But how can I respect someone who seemingly has no respect for himself? And how can I respect someone who at times seems so unworthy of my respect?

Let us put this in perspective.

I must remember first of all that my husband, though degraded by alcohol and sin, has a living soul. Jesus loves him and died for him. I must also keep in mind my husband's future potential, if he can be brought to accept the salvation Jesus offers. Surely if Jesus loves my alcoholic husband I can do no less. Because Jesus does love him and seeks to show that love *through* me, I must love, honor, and respect him.

Paul tells us that love never fails (1 Corinthians 13:8). I used to think this meant love always accomplishes its objective. However, it could mean that our source of love is inexhaustible; it will never run dry. That will be true as long as we depend on the God of love as our source of love.

Paul states another principle for us to follow: "Wives, submit yourselves unto your own husbands, as unto the Lord. For the husband is the head of the wife, even as Christ is the head of the church. . . . Therefore as the church is subject unto Christ, so let the wives be to their own husbands in every thing" (Ephesians 5:22-24).

Did you notice that Paul did not qualify this command? He did not say, "Now wives, submit as long as your husbands are kind and gentle." He said, "Submit . . . in everything, just as the church obeys Christ in all things."

I hear someone objecting, "Do you mean I actually have to submit to that brute?"

Yes, you do. But when you truly submit, you will no longer see your husband as a brute, regardless of his conduct. Because submission without meekness is impossible, I have emphasized strongly in previous chapters the spiritual resources necessary to live with an alcoholic.

Submission has a powerful influence. Much, but not all, of the conflict that develops between the alcoholic and his family takes place because other family members react adversely to him and the effects of alcohol on his personality. If the wife can submit to her husband's whims, she removes the source of conflict and avoids the war!

One Sunday morning in March, just before I left for church, Gene noticed an article in *Grit* (a weekly family newspaper) about a wildflower retreat scheduled for a weekend in April. It took place at Blackwater Falls near Davis, West Virginia, about a three-hour drive from our home.

Gene and I shared a love for wildflowers. He suggested we plan to go to Blackwater Falls on Sunday. Naturally, I wanted to attend church on Sunday, so I opted for Saturday. We jockeyed for position, each arguing for the merits of our day. I made the mistake of telling Gene that I saw through what we were doing: we were trying to manipulate each other to get our own way.

Gene exploded in anger. He informed me, "If that is the way you're going to act, you can just stay at home today! You're not going out that door."

I quietly handed him the keys to the car. "All right," I replied calmly. "We'll stay at home then." I laid aside my Bible and purse and removed my coat. I prepared, without anger or bitterness, to remain at home.

Gene ranted and raved for a few minutes. I did not answer him or argue with him. I merely listened respectfully. Finally he tossed me the car keys. He swore fiercely, telling me to take the keys and go to church. I thanked him and the Lord and went to church.

While we are commanded to submit to our husbands, we must also be as "bold as a lion" (Proverbs 28:1) in standing up for what is right when a clear line of distinction exists. Acts 5:29 says, "We ought to obey God rather than men." If what our husbands ask of us conflicts with what the Lord requires, our first loyalty rests in obeying God. This sometimes demands great courage.

Gene served as jack-of-all-trades for widows and elderly people in the community. He cleaned cisterns and painted roofs. He refinished the interior surfaces of houses and performed a host of other odd jobs about the Glen.

Gene expected me to file our income tax report. But this developed a sore spot between us. When I filed our first income tax forms after my recommitment to Christ, I included an estimated sum of $200 as income received by Gene for his odd jobs. He became very angry, not because the sum was too high, but because I had reported this income. He made it loud and clear that under no circumstances was I to do that again.

It bothered me that Gene refused to let me report any income over and above his normal wages. I felt I was being dishonest in signing forms when I knew the figures were not correct. I begged him to take the tax forms to a professional, but he refused. I had to fill them in.

After talking this over with a wise elderly friend, I concluded that my position must be somewhat similar to that of Naaman after being healed of leprosy. He said to Elisha, "In this thing the LORD pardon thy servant, that when my master goeth into the house of Rimmon to worship there, and he leaneth on my hand, and I bow myself in the house of Rimmon: when I bow down myself in the house of Rimmon, the LORD pardon thy servant in this thing. And he [Elisha] said unto him, Go in peace" (2 Kings 5:18, 19).

Naaman did not want to be in the house of Rimmon, but he had no choice. His master required his presence there; and as one under authority, Naaman had to obey. Naaman determined, however, that he personally would worship only the God of Israel.

The solution I settled on was simple. I decided to report every penny of my earnings. The Lord would hold Gene responsible for his.

This conclusion agrees with a Scripture I later discovered. "If a woman also vow a vow unto the LORD, . . . And if she had at all an husband, when she vowed, . . . and [if] her husband heard it, and held his peace at her in the day that he heard it: then her vows shall stand" (Numbers 30:3, 6, 7). An example of this would be Hannah in her prayer for a child. She vowed to return the child to the Lord after praying for a son (1 Samuel 1:11). Elkanah allowed that vow to stand "in the day that he heard it" (see 1 Samuel 1:21-23).

Numbers 30 continues: "But if her husband disallowed her on the day that he heard it; then he shall make her vow which she vowed . . . of none effect: and the LORD shall forgive her. . . . her husband hath made them void; and the LORD shall forgive her. . . . But if he shall any ways make them void . . . he [the husband] shall bear her iniquity" (verses 8, 12, 15).

This passage fit my position exactly. I had determined to be honest in tax reporting, but my husband "disallowed" it; he overruled me. The Lord would require an accounting from him.

This resolution of the problem on my part did not end the conflict, however. Gene hated paying income taxes, especially if our deductions had not covered the amount of our tax. I dreaded filling in the forms because of his predictable anger, either because our refund was too small or because the amount we had to pay was too large.

Although Gene tolerated my inclusion of the few dollars I had earned, he deeply resented it. In his view this raised the amount he had to pay, and that irked him. One year he moodily entered the living room after I had presented the forms to him for his signature. He glanced at the gun rack on the wall and remarked, "I know one way I could take care of it."

I understood what he was thinking. He could shoot me, and he would no longer need to cope with my tender conscience! The Lord gave me perfect peace. I answered calmly, "You mean you'd do all that for just a few dollars?" He wilted and that ended the problem.

Another incident demanding the "boldness of a lion" occurred after Keith, our youngest, entered school.

Gene insisted I find a job. This prospect concerned me because I saw the potential for trouble. I could not allow Gene to use my wages for alcohol, but I knew he would resent separate checking accounts. What was I to do?

The state employment agency sent me to check a position with an optometrist who sought a receptionist-bookkeeper. But I lacked the bookkeeping skills he wanted.

Next the employment commission directed me to a local grocery store that needed an additional checkout clerk. I had never been in this store. As I walked in, I showed the clerk the slip from the agency, and he told me to wait. The boss would be in soon.

As I waited to be interviewed, I browsed through the aisles with the idea of comparing prices with my store, since the two were competitors. I did not reach the end of the first aisle before one section stopped me cold.

What should I do? I looked at the six-packs of beer and the bottles of wine on the shelves. I thought of ringing up those mind-twisting drugs on the cash register and sending them out into homes where mothers and children would suffer because of my action. I considered the heartache I would bring into those homes. I recalled Habakkuk 2:15 —"Woe unto him that giveth his neighbour drink"—but I also anticipated Gene's anger. I knew my decision, based solely on the grounds of a refusal to sell alcoholic beverages, would not please him.

Another element, however, entered my consideration. What right would I have to condemn Gene's addiction if I sold alcoholic drinks to others? What would passing this product through my cash register do to my testimony?

I returned to the clerk I had spoken with when I had entered the store. "I'm sorry," I said sincerely, "but I can't work here. I didn't know you sold alcoholic beverages."

My refusal to even consider this opening made Gene furious. I stood my ground, however, and his anger eventually cooled. Sometime later I sold my first story, and with the launching of my career as an author, Gene no longer insisted I find outside work.

Little things sometimes became as hard to knuckle down to as the bigger ones. If I planned to plant peas on the upper edge of the garden, Gene insisted on the lower. (*He doesn't take care of the garden anyway; I do!* I fumed to myself, but that was not quite true. Gene did work hard trying to control the bindweed in our vegetable garden.) Or perhaps Gene pressured me into riding into town with him when I had decided to do the laundry.

I discovered, however, that the Lord held great blessings in reserve for me when I humbled myself and submitted to Gene's requests.

Sometimes on that trip to town I would run into a good friend whom I had not seen in years. Or I would find a rare flower while accompanying Gene to the woods when I really did not want to go. The Lord always blessed me when I humbled myself and did as my husband wished. Sometimes the blessing came in just knowing that I had pleased my Lord by being obedient to His will.

Peter presents the matter of submission in a different light. He puts it this way: "Likewise, ye wives, be in subjection to your own husbands; that, if any obey not the word, they also may without the word be won by the conversation [manner of life] of the wives; while they behold your chaste conversation coupled with fear" (1 Peter 3:1, 2).

Notice that Peter addresses wives whose husbands "obey not the word." That's us! Furthermore, Peter tells us our husbands will be won by our modest conduct. On one occasion while my husband still drank heavily, I had the opportunity to check this Scripture in several different versions. To my amazement, each version rendered it the same way. The husband would be won, without a word from his wife, by her godly life.

At first I understood this to mean that my husband would be saved, and for some that may be true. For me it meant that I won his respect, cooperation, and sobriety.

I found that Scripture very comforting. I no longer felt compelled to witness verbally to Gene. Nor did I leave tracts and books in obvious places for him to read. (He never touched them anyway.) I could relax in the knowledge that my everyday living was speaking for me.

Peter offers further advice on how to behave. He counsels: "Whose adorning let it not be that outward adorning of plaiting the hair, and of wearing of gold, or of putting on of apparel; but let it be the hidden man of the heart, in that which is not corruptible, even the ornament of a meek and quiet spirit, which is in the sight of God of great price" (1 Peter 3:3, 4).

Submission that does not spring from a meek and quiet spirit accomplishes little. I found a statement in a dictionary of Bible words that struck me. "Meekness," this author insists, "is the fruit of power." The meek person can only exercise that virtue because the indwelling power of the Holy Spirit enables her to respond in love rather than wrath. It allows her to submit instead of demanding her own way. Without the Holy Spirit she has no source of strength on which to draw, and she retaliates in anger and bitterness.

My pastor says he is amazed at the places Gene took me. Although I looked and dressed quite differently from the wives of his friends, he actually seemed to enjoy showing me off. I never understood why.

When I attended these functions with Gene—his army reunion, for example—Gene left me alone while he wandered off in search of his buddies. I had two choices: I could sit around and choose to be miserable, or I could make friends of my own. I chose the latter. I set out to build friendships with the strangers among whom I found myself. The Lord blessed these efforts, and I soon looked forward to seeing my friends at these yearly gatherings.

Coming back to the subject of gardening—a perennial pest exists in our garden. Bindweed is a tough vine with roots that burrow deep into the red clay soil. I know of no one who has successfully eradicated it. It belongs to the morning glory family and is known locally as bindvine.

Gene despised this weed. He fought it continually. He especially resented its presence among my dahlia plants where it could not be hoed off. The weed had to be separated from the dahlia stalks and pulled out by hand.

One day Gene stormed into the house. "If you don't get that old green vine out of your dahlias," he raged, "I will. I'll spray it with kerosene; then I know I'll have it!"

I took Gene's threat seriously. I dropped what I was doing, donned my sunbonnet, and collected my gardening tools. I began the task of extracting that troublesome vine from among my flowers. Gene must have regretted his outburst; he soon started the garden tiller and joined me in cleaning up the dahlia row.

In spite of the bindvine, Gene's attitude toward my dahlias changed in the next few years and he voluntarily helped me plant the bulbs. In fact, he took pride in the dahlia row and sometimes de-vined it himself.

Admittedly, submitting to an alcoholic husband is not easy, but it produces the joy of God's approval. Although Gene did not become a Christian, I believe he stopped drinking because God gave me the grace to submit.

10. What Can I Do?

Life seems to be full of hard knocks. Taunts and insults rock our spirits. For the wife of the alcoholic, this trauma comes, not from outside the home, but from her own husband—perhaps not always, but far too often. What can she do about it? Can anything be done to improve her marriage?

The first thing I must do to improve my marriage and my circumstances is to learn to forgive. Trying to reason with a person under the influence of alcohol accomplishes nothing. He may make promises when sober, but alcohol quickly inhibits his ability to keep those pledges. I learned I could not expect sane, rational behavior from Gene when he was drinking. Since I could do nothing to change his action, I had to overlook it and forgive him.

I do not mean to imply that we should not talk over problems with our husbands when they are sober. We need to. I recall a trip I wanted to make to northwestern Ontario in connection with a forthcoming book I was writing. I planned to travel with my son Dennis and my nephew Russ. After returning home from previous journeys to the area, Gene had attached evil motives to my going, although he knew the travel was necessary to my work as an author.

When I asked Gene about continuing north after attending a wedding in Indiana, he readily consented. Before I left I also got him to agree not to falsely accuse me when I returned.

The confrontational method of handling problems may not be best for you. I used it because I knew Gene. If humble, quiet confrontation does not avert false accusation, we may ask the Lord for grace to exercise forbearance and forgiveness.

Confronting our spouses with difficulties while they are sober reminds me of Abigail, the wife of Nabal (1 Samuel 25). David asked Nabal for food for his army because his men had protected Nabal's flocks and herds when David's men had been in Carmel. When Nabal rebuffed David's messengers and treated them roughly, David determined to take revenge.

A servant told Abigail about this and warned her to act quickly. She loaded bread, wine, dressed sheep, roasted grain, raisins, and figs onto donkeys and rode out to meet David. Her prompt action prevented bloodshed. But because Nabal was drunk, she did not tell him what she had done until the next morning, when he was sober. A wise woman and a good example for us!

Forgiveness is possible for us only if we have been forgiven. In the early days of our marriage, I often said "I'm sorry" to restore peace when I felt the fault had not been mine. I did not forgive Gene. Forgiveness frees the other person from guilt or blame. I did not free Gene, for in my heart I still held him responsible.

I now understand that I could not forgive until I had experienced forgiveness through Jesus. In those days I was probably a lot more to blame for our conflicts than I realized.

During the seven years we provided a home for Gene's mother, the necessity to forgive was constant. Almost every Sunday evening Gene sat in the kitchen talking to Granny. I heard a continual stream of criticism about "the old woman" (me) and Granny's cluck of agreement. Gene once told me, "I like to talk to Granny; she agrees with me." In such instances I needed to forgive both of them!

I do not recall how Gene met Jim, a man who had lost a leg above the knee because of gangrene and was bedridden. Both Jim and his housekeeper, Susie, were alcoholics. Gene spent a lot of time with Jim and Susie and frequently stopped by our house with Susie when going to or from town.

In the old days I would have been wild with jealousy and concern. Not now! Forgiveness enabled me to be a witness to Jim and Susie. Although I had not known Jim previously, his minister father had accompanied us on our first Sunday morning trip to the mountains when I was a child. So when one Saturday evening Gene asked me to visit Jim with him, I went.

Jim seemed pleased to see me. We talked about his father and reminisced about the "good old days." I reminded Jim of his need to get right with the Lord. Although Jim knew he needed to do this, he was not ready to take that step. He readily agreed that I could pray for him, which I did.

While Jim and Gene chatted, I sat down to talk with Susie. When I told her about Jesus I soon sensed a deep spiritual hunger and a real desire to be free from her current lifestyle. She willingly agreed to pray with me, but when I suggested we kneel beside the sofa to pray, she balked. I did not press the matter. If Susie was not ready to bend her knees, she probably had not humbled her heart.

Following that visit I continued to intercede for Jim and Susie. Our group at prayer meeting also prayed for Jim since some in the group knew Jim's family. I also accompanied Gene to the hospital to visit Jim. When Jim asked me to sing, "Take the Name of Jesus With You," I complied, although my voice leaves much to be desired. In spite of our prayers and our combined efforts, Jim passed into eternity without hope.

Susie called me one summer day and asked me to take her into the city for medicine. I quizzed her sharply about this because I knew how devious alcoholics can be. She insisted that the doctor had given her a prescription she needed to have filled.

Grave doubts about her truthfulness, however, lingered in my mind, but at last I agreed to drive to her home. I emphasized that I was only coming to check out the situation, and that my presence there would not be a guarantee that I would take her to town!

When I arrived, Susie rushed out of the house, prepared to leave immediately for the city.

"What medicine do you need, Susie?" I probed.

"I've got to have something for a cold," Susie hedged.

I knew all about "cold medicine." Gene had introduced it to me years ago.

"Susie," I insisted, "I want to see your prescription."

Susie patted a pocket on her dress. "I've got it right here," she declared.

I repeated, "Susie, show me the prescription.

Instead she whined, "You said you would take me into town."

"No, Susie," I replied firmly. "I told you I would come to your house. I didn't promise to take you to town." I added, "I'm sorry, Susie, but I can't take you to get anything to drink. You know that."

When it became obvious to Susie that her attempt had failed, she stomped back into the house and I returned home.

On those occasions when Susie and Gene stopped by the house, I often played the old hymns of the faith on our reed organ. Susie loved to listen to them.

One Sunday afternoon I played "My Faith Looks Up to Thee." Susie became very agitated and said, "Oh, no, no! Don't play that one!"

"But why?" I asked, confused by her reaction.

"It's a death song," Susie replied, wringing her hands. "They sing it at funerals."

"Yes," I answered, "but it is what I live by."

Susie once told me, "I like to come to your house."

"Do you know why you like to come to my house?" I asked.

"Yes," she replied. "It's because God is there."

I pondered what my attitude toward Susie would have been had not "God been there." I thanked Him that forgiveness turns a potential tragedy into the opportunity for witness.

The Lord also used my witness to Susie in another way.

Gene told me in one of our Saturday night confrontations prior to Susie's death, "I propositioned Susie once, and she slapped me in the face."

How I praised God! Had I not prayed for Susie, witnessed to her, and tried to love her into the kingdom, that episode could have ended quite differently. I reasoned at the time that Susie had too much respect for me to agree to what Gene asked of her.

Susie died some years later in a tragic automobile accident. I thanked God that He had given me the opportunity to love her and to witness to her of His saving grace. She, however, chose to reject that grace and entered eternity unprepared.

I recall only once when Gene offhandedly asked me to forgive him. It happened on Memorial Day 1970. I have already alluded to this incident and cannot relate the details out of respect for my husband. At that time he said, "If you don't forgive me, it's over for us." I forgave him.

More often than not, our spouses probably do not realize they have hurt us. Unless we forgive these little insults and injuries as they occur, the pressure builds up. The resulting explosion will cause deeper hurts, more difficult to heal.

One method I have used in coping with untrue accusations may be useful to others. If, for example, Gene charged me with engaging in an affair rather than going to church and he refused to drop the matter, I sometimes effectually closed the subject by saying quietly and sincerely, "I forgive you for accusing me falsely."

At times it seemed to me that I had to do all the forgiving, but there were incidents when I needed to say, "I'm sorry. I shouldn't have said that." I should have added more often than I did, "Will you forgive me?"

Jesus makes forgiveness imperative. Unless we forgive others, in this case our husbands, He will not forgive us. And who among us does not need to be forgiven?

Besides forgiving our husbands for the hurts and aches their addiction brings into our lives, are there other things we can do to build a better marriage? Yes, definitely!

Enjoy together the things you can. Because you may have a different set of friends and go separate ways much of the time, doing things together which both you and your husband enjoy becomes doubly important.

We must also make the best of the good times. In our family, the good times were times of togetherness as a family.

I recall a trip to the lake country of northwestern Ontario. Erma had registered for a voluntary service term as a Bible school teacher among Native Americans. I wanted Gene to make the journey and take her there because I felt sure he would love the wide, uncluttered country.

Gene was determined not to go. I think he feared the spiritual atmosphere he expected to find there. Nevertheless, the Lord altered Gene's thinking, and he decided to make the trip.

While in the area I wanted to interview one of the missionaries for information I needed for one of my books. In order to see this individual, the mission plane had to fly Gene and me into the Indian reservation where he was located.

The plane that transported us from Red Lake to Deer Lake was a small pontooned one that seated about eight people. How Gene enjoyed that flight! He reminded me of a small boy with a new toy. He seemed determined to learn everything about the operation of the plane. He watched the dials on the instrument panel and observed how the plane responded to various signals from the pilot. Gene's eyes eagerly scanned the forest and lakes below for moose.

A wind developed during the ninety-minute flight, and by the time we landed on Deer Lake, soft, white-capped waves ruffled its surface.

We had planned to stay on the reservation only long enough to conduct the interview. The wind, however, increased and for four days continued to whip the waters of the lake into frothy waves. It was impossible for a plane to come in for us since it could not land on the choppy lake.

As our missionary host asked one man after another from meal to meal to ask the blessing on the food, I sensed Gene's deep uneasiness. I knew he worried about when his turn would come! I mentioned this privately to our host, and suddenly Gene relaxed. I am not sure what happened—whether our host and I both prayed about it, or whether Roy spoke to Gene. From that day on Gene's tenseness vanished, and he enjoyed his stay in the bush. He occupied his time by helping to build a road on the reservation, a task in which his knowledge proved very useful.

I filled my hours by helping the missionary's wife with the laundry and the ironing. (Electricity was supplied by a generator.) I also helped with the cooking, cleaning, and dishwashing.

Gene loved bush life. He even found good words to say of our missionary host.

When Erma later returned to work for a year at this

same mission, Gene and I took the boys up to see her. We explored a gold mine and fished in one of the quiet lakes. Erma snared her hand with a fishhook during that outing. Since we were too far from civilization for a quick dash to the doctor, Gene expertly disengaged the hook with his pocketknife.

Evidence of how much Gene enjoyed the north country emerged when we prepared to bring Erma home after her term of service ended. Two of Gene's friends, also employees of the highway department, decided to accompany us! Gene had talked so enthusiastically about the north that Jack and Rodney wanted to see it too.

Gene and I drove our car while Jack, Rodney, and their wives traveled in another. We led the way and they attempted to follow us, which was not easy since our car was more powerful than theirs and Gene liked speed!

This journey took place in late March. At that time of the year, northwestern Ontario is still snowy, cold, and frozen. This did not discourage Gene's friends. They accompanied Gene and Erma on a snowmobile trip into the bush in search of a willow log Gene wanted. Erma accidentally dumped Jack into the snow when she put the vehicle into gear just as Jack prepared to sit down! That was something to joke about for years afterward.

The wives, Nancy and Linda, adored the black-eyed Indian babies and wished they could take them along home. And for years Jack spoke of returning to the area for a summer fishing trip, although that never happened.

As mentioned earlier, Gene remained sober while traveling. We welcomed the beauty and calmness of those days which seemed like an oasis in the desert. Those times helped to restore the cohesiveness of the family and to heal hurts from other less peaceful times.

Our traveling days also permitted us freedom from

the tension of Gene's unpredictable behavior. During this short period of time, we could be assured we would face no embarrassment and no crises due to his addiction. Over the years Gene and I made four trips to Red Lake.

Many of the happy times our family experienced stemmed from our mutual love for the mountains. Because Gene grew up in a remote highland area, he had acquired an abundant knowledge of his surroundings.

For example, Gene knew which plants were edible and which ones could be brewed for tea. He knew which acorn trees produced sweet nuts and which trees produced bitter nuts. He also recognized which trees made the best firewood and which ones to harvest for chair splints or fence posts.

Gene had a deep love for wild creatures. I marveled at his ability to walk into the forest and "read" it from the evidence he found: the spoor of different animals; their prints in the soft earth; the scars on trees left by bear, deer, or moose; the plants nipped off by browsing deer. To Gene, each of these told its own story.

Gene had a keen sense of direction. Many times he parked the pickup at the edge of an unfamiliar woods and after scouting the area for deer sign or mushrooms he returned unerringly to his vehicle. This knack for getting around in the forest proved useful in gathering mushrooms. Gene grew up eating this delicacy and he and the boys spent many summer afternoons searching the woods for them.

I admired Gene's knowledge of individual trees. He recognized them by their shape as well as by their bark. He could identify trees in their stark winter austerity or when clothed with summer green, be they oak, maple, poplar, or birch.

This ability to sort out different trees became a boost to our family when our children entered high school.

One biology assignment consisted of making and identifying a collection of leaves. I still remember those leaf-collecting excursions as a pleasant time of family togetherness.

Before Granny came to live with us, we enjoyed driving in the country. Gene liked the challenge of an unfamiliar road. He took them to see where they "came out."

One Sunday afternoon while investigating an unpaved road east of Massanutten Mountain, a landmark in the Shenandoah Valley, we discovered a restored iron furnace. I also found a new flower, a purple member of the pea family, which I have not seen since.

That Sunday afternoon a thunderstorm unexpectedly drenched the boys riding in the back of the truck, although Erma, Gene, and I remained cozy and dry in the cab. It turned out to be a memorable day!

Sometimes Gene prepared a picnic lunch for us on Sunday while we were in church. Then we would drive into the mountains for a Sunday afternoon picnic. In those days several fire towers still existed in the surrounding mountains. These towers were built as lookouts for fire and were staffed during the summer when fires were most likely to occur. I detest heights, but Gene and the children frequently scrambled to the top of the towers.

During the years when my parents conducted Sunday school in the highland churches, I learned to appreciate wildflowers. My father purchased a wildflower encyclopedia that accompanied us each Sunday just as faithfully as Bibles and flannelgraph materials.

Gene encouraged this interest in wildflowers. Nearly every spring we loaded the children into the back of the pickup, often with some of their friends from church, and took a long drive into the mountains to search for flowers. The children learned to appreciate and recognize many of our native species during those outings.

I remember one Sunday afternoon when Gene returned carrying a beautiful pink flower with a distinctive shape. He proudly presented it to me and asked me what it was.

I answered promptly, "It's a shooting star."

Disappointed, he said, "Oh! I thought I had really found something."

"You did," I assured him. "It is the first one I have ever seen."

"Then how did you know what it was?" he demanded.

I explained that in constantly leafing through the encyclopedia to identify other flowers, I had seen this one and recognized it when he handed it to me. He understood.

When I asked Gene where he had found the shooting star, he said Jim had wanted to go for a drive to visit the old home place, which lies on the ridge of mountains that forms the Virginia-West Virginia boundary line. Gene discovered the shooting star on this trip.

I learned to cooperate with my husband when I could. The children and I never lingered to talk after the benediction on Sunday morning. Soon after we left the house to go to church on Sunday morning, Gene would begin preparing dinner for us. Consequently, if we stayed after church to visit, by the time we returned home, his meat loaf, fried potatoes, tomato gravy, and green beans had cooled and had to be reheated. No cook likes to warm up food, so we usually rushed home.

On rare occasions we did not arrive home after church services as quickly as Gene thought we should. That caused problems, but we tried to bear patiently with his tantrums. How many other wives whose husbands refused to attend church with them would have dinner ready for them when they returned? That we could almost predict the menu made no difference. Gene was a good cook—better than I, he said—and that probably was true.

When Gene asked me to fix the sagging ceiling of our sedan, I did it. (Never mind how it looked!) When he insisted I accompany him to his army reunion, I cheerfully went, although I felt totally out of place. When he invited me to a country music sing and dance, however, I declined.

I always felt uneasy riding with Gene while he was driving under the influence of alcohol. I look back and wonder what I could or perhaps should have done differently. I do praise God for His mercy. Gene never had a serious accident when driving while drinking. Surely the Lord protected us and the other drivers on the road.

My friend Mary refuses to ride with her husband when she knows he is drinking. Recently Mary and Dick decided to visit their son. After traveling for some time, Dick produced a bottle of wine from under the seat and proceeded to take a swallow. Mary faced him squarely. "Take me home, Dick," she said firmly. "I didn't know you had that bottle when I agreed to go to see Sandy." Dick took her home.

Gene would not have done the same for me. Such a request probably would have caused him to become stubborn and would have placed us in physical danger.

In closing this chapter I must say again, Remember to be thankful. Thank God for the times of togetherness that you and your children enjoy with your husband. If you do not have any such activities, try to find some in which you can participate as a family.

You might enjoy jigsaw puzzles, making popcorn balls, or reading aloud. Before Gene purchased the television, he and I spent many Sunday afternoons challenging each other at checkers. Erma, Keith, and I thrive on Scrabble. The Lord will lead you to your family activity if you ask Him. And when He does, do not forget to thank Him!

11. You and Your Children

Children of an alcoholic father live in troubling circumstances. The rules may not be consistent; what applied one weekend may not be what is expected the next. The children never know when an innocent remark will ignite a spark that will flare into a full-blown tantrum. Violence erupts unexpectedly, and they may be punished unfairly.

What part do we as mothers play in this scenario? How can we help? How do we cope with injustice and changing rules?

I found that filling the role of mother was perhaps the most arduous task that fell to me as the wife of an alcoholic. Washing dishes and laundering clothes affect little the spiritual welfare of our children. Finances perish and money carries no eternal value, but the souls of our children live forever. What I do with the opportunity given me may later determine their eternal destiny.

After renewing my covenant with the Lord, I developed a concern for my family. Immediately I checked our church library for books I could use in devotions with the children. Few such books existed. A dear friend, however, purchased a devotional book for me which our children thoroughly enjoyed. The boys were not satisfied for me to read the entry for one day only; I usually read several. They also loved the exploits of David, Joseph, Daniel, and even Jeremiah, which I read directly from my Bible. About this time also, we began asking the blessing before meals—a brief, simple prayer.

When we started attending a small church nearer home, the boys devoured the children's books in the church library. As finances permitted I purchased new books from the Christian book racks in my grocery store. Nearly every evening Leonard came with a book and asked me to read it.

In addition to instruction in spiritual values, these reading times proved worthwhile in another way. After Keith started school, his progress in reading amazed me. I asked him where he learned all the words he recognized.

"Why, Mama," he replied matter-of-factly. "I just watch when you are reading to us, and when you come to a word I don't know, I find out what it is."

Those evening reading sessions ended when Gene brought in the television. I objected strenuously to the entrance of television into our home, but I knew that to express that objection too verbally to Gene would produce a result opposite of what I wished. So instead of arguing against it, I applied other tactics.

When Gene stated one morning that he planned to get a TV that weekend, I replied, "I'm not going to try to stop you, but I am going to ask the Lord to." And I did. I do not know what method the Lord used to alter Gene's thinking, but no television appeared at that time.

About six months later Gene again announced his intention of buying a television. I did not say anything to him. Instead, I asked several friends to pray with me about it.

This time Gene did purchase a television set. Since I know that lack of faith on our part did not hinder the answer to our prayers, I must conclude the Lord had His reasons for allowing Gene to buy the television. Gene did hear the Gospel many times over the years through this medium.

After Gene's death I disposed of the television since I had no use for it.

Besides being responsible for the spiritual nurture of their children, another hurdle wives of alcoholics face concerns the attitude of their children toward their fathers. Children "catch" the mood of their parents. We teach, most often, when we are unaware of our instruction. If we model love, honor, and respect for our husbands, our children will likely copy it.

For children to understand that they must love, honor, and respect a father who abuses them requires first of all a stalwart, living example from their mother! She must model love, honor, and respect in the face of verbal or physical abuse if her children are to show their father proper respect.

I have had to work through bouts of anger and frustration with my children caused by Gene's addiction. Sometimes Gene in his twisted thinking leveled unjust accusations at them or he disciplined them too severely (which he never undertook unless drunk). In such cases I needed to act as a mediator.

"But why?" you ask. "Why honor a father who abuses you? Does God really expect it?"

Yes, He does. "Honour thy father and thy mother" (Exodus 20:12). The Lord does not say, "Honor your father if he is decent and kind." The Lord places no limitations on His command. Paul echoes the order in his Epistles (Ephesians 6:2).

Why must our children honor an alcoholic who, in our human way of thinking, deserves no honor? Simply because he is their father. The first command the Lord lays down for children is that they honor their parents whom God has placed over them.

I mentioned in an earlier chapter the problem I had one Sunday morning when Gene told Leonard he did not have to go to church, and Leonard did not go. I realized at the time that how I approached that situation could be the difference of eternity for our son.

I prayed much about it and the Lord brought the solution to my mind. I could not contradict my husband's headship but must manage the problem from a different angle. One day when my son and I were alone, I explained, "Leonard, I know Daddy told you that you don't have to go to church if you don't want to, but **I'm** expecting you to go."

When I decided to deal with the situation from this angle, I also determined to pray earnestly that the Lord would move this son of mine to obey. Leonard continued to attend church until he purchased his own car.

An approach such as this will not succeed unless you have earned the respect of your children through consistent discipline over a period of years.

Prayer is indispensable in coping with the friction produced by alcohol. We must pray for our children as well as for our husbands.

Will the boys follow the example of their alcoholic father or will they choose to walk in their mother's footsteps? I read a statement during those early years that chilled my heart: "Boys will love their mothers, but they will follow their fathers." I redoubled my prayers, but in my case the prediction proved true for a time. I am still pleading with the Lord for the salvation of two of my sons.

Since I believed in the old saying, Idleness is the devil's workshop, I tried to keep my children occupied, especially during the summer months. I required them to help in the garden and with the laundry, the cooking, and the canning. After all, Paul says, "If any would not work, neither should he eat" (2 Thessalonians 3:10). Paul does not limit this command to adults!

To this day, when my family gathers I find myself hunting for something for my children to do if they begin picking at one another. Old habits die hard!

Dennis especially enjoyed helping in the kitchen. He baked apple pies, sugar cookies, and pound cake. Also he treated the family to apple roll-ups, a form of apple dumplings, for dessert. His expertise extended to serving sourdough buckwheat cakes for breakfast at the youth overnight campout. I greatly missed Dennis if for some reason he needed to be elsewhere during meal preparation.

All the children loved to help me make bread dough. Erma learned the process, start to finish, but the boys usually started the dough before they left for school. They knew how much warm water, yeast, sugar, salt, and shortening to measure into my mixing container. They added flour, stirring the dough with a wooden paddle until it became stiff. When the dough reached the consistency of being too heavy to stir, they placed a lid on the pan, and I finished it later.

I also attempted to teach responsibility. Our boys were the only youths available to mow lawns around the Glen. They usually had several yards that needed to be done at the same time. These had to be finished before they could have free time.

Dennis enjoyed garden work and frequently helped some of the widows in the village with their gardens.

Leonard told me recently he wishes I would have insisted the children save their money. He says he knows they would have moaned and complained, but he can now see the value of the saving habit.

Why did my children not learn to save? I am not sure why I neglected to teach this virtue. Maybe I was too tired from coping with other problems that seemed more important. I now recognize, however, that the results would have been worth the trouble.

The crisis permitting the boys the freedom to go their own way came in May 1974, when my father developed gangrene in his right foot. Papa spent sixteen weeks at the University of Virginia Hospital in Charlottesville, Virginia. During that period he underwent two amputations on his right leg. Since I am the only child in Virginia, I felt the need to help my parents whenever a crisis occurred.

Because Mama was unable to stay alone, I dropped everything to care for her. Granny Crider still remained well enough then to cook for my family while I stayed with my mother. My father's sister frequently relieved me on weekends, permitting me to come home for a day or two. Eventually my sister arranged to come from Pennsylvania to stay with Mama for several weeks, and finally our sixteen-year-old niece arrived to remain until school began.

While I was away caring for Mama, the boys were left unsupervised for long periods of time, and they did as they pleased. They experimented with a host of evils: alcohol, immorality, and drugs. While my presence at home may not have altered the final outcome, my absence hastened their downfall. I believe the boys were into evil habits before my father's hospitalization, but lack of supervision opened the door to greater involvement.

Circumstances producing grave consequences developed from Gene's refusal to accept Dennis as his son. I still remember the Sunday afternoon when Gene took Leonard and Keith with him in the pickup and left Dennis crying in the yard. This rejection continued and eventually Dennis got the message.

In the summer of 1975, when Dennis was 19 years of age, he chose to rebel. I am not sure whether Gene accepted Dennis as his son at this time, although he could hardly escape the evidence. Even the neighbors talked about it. Although in physical appearance Dennis resembled my side of the family, in his manner of doing things such as hoeing weeds, digging potatoes, operating the garden tiller, and in his mechanical ability, he mirrored Gene precisely.

A heart attack two years before had almost taken

Gene's life. I had hoped it would bring about his sobriety, but it did not. After the scare wore thin, he had begun drinking again.

Gene remained sober for eight weeks in the summer of 1975. The boys overheard him tell a friend who offered him a beer, "I'd better leave that stuff alone. My heart has been skipping beats."

The situation that erupted in July 1975, however, taxed his ability to cope, and he returned to alcohol. He explained later that his "nerves were shot and that tranquilizers no longer helped." He had not wanted to yield to his old habit.

On the evening of July 28, 1975, Dennis came downstairs carrying a box. "What are you doing?" I inquired.

The smile Dennis pitched my way puzzled me. It reminded me of the times when as a small boy he was contemplating mischief. "You'll find out," he answered.

Dennis did not return home that night, nor the next, or the night after that. We learned from his employer that he had not been at work. We learned also that Dennis's friend Bob and Bob's girlfriend Judy were also missing. We surmised they were together somewhere.

Gene's attitude disturbed me. "I'll bet he's really gotten himself into trouble this time," he gloated. "He needn't come to me for help."

About three weeks passed before we heard from the young people. In the meantime we discovered that the group had not left with empty pockets. Judy had contributed $300 from her wages, and Dennis had cashed his paycheck at a gas station enroute to Interstate 81.

During this three-week period, the time arrived and passed for Dennis to make a payment on his car. Gene talked to the loan officer at the bank. "We can report the car stolen," the official informed Gene. "Dennis wasn't supposed to leave the state with the car without our permission and without yours since you signed the note for him."

Bob called home August 16, telling his family that he and his friends were in Texas. He said they were living in a park equipped with shelters (picnic tables, we later learned!) and had received several job offers, but none they chose to accept.

Bob's mother told us also that Bob wanted to know what the authorities were doing about him, since he had walked away from a juvenile detention center. Bob informed her that he intended to remain free until his eighteenth birthday and then return to school.

Dennis phoned collect shortly after we received the call from Bob's mother. I reminded him of the car payment and also told him of the fine print in his contract with the bank. He promised to send the payment as soon as possible.

He added jovially, before hanging up, "I'll see you in a year, maybe."

Good! I thought. *You can learn a lot in that time and unlearn a lot you think you know.*

In the meantime we discovered that two sleeping bags were also missing from our storage area. That explained how the group could sleep in the park.

Although Bob had told his family that the young people were in Texas, we were not sure we could believe him. Bob's word lacked credibility, for good reason.

In a roundabout way we learned also that Judy wished to come home. Word reached us that her parents were considering a trip to Texas to bring her back.

I personally believed the Lord had more He wanted to accomplish in the lives of these young people before bringing them home. That gave me peace.

About August 30, 1975, Bob's mother phoned again. She said Bob had called from Texas. Dennis and Jim, another member of the party, had been arrested and were in jail. Bob, Judy, and Jim, all juveniles, were to be flown back to Virginia. Dennis would remain in jail and face charges there. Bob informed his mother that Dennis planned to fight the charge.

Gene actually looked happy when he heard our son was in jail awaiting trial.

Because the car Dennis drove to Texas belonged to the bank, someone had to bring it back. Gene decided to go for it himself. He planned to take Erma and one of her friends along, a young lady aspiring to be a social worker.

This did not set too well with me. I felt as the mother of the person involved it should be my right to go. Gene insisted I would try to help Dennis. Erma's friend, who believes strongly in allowing persons to reap the consequences of their actions, turned to me and asked, "Would you [try to help him]?"

I answered, "I don't know; it depends on what I find when I get there."

That exchange prompted me to pray fervently that the Lord would intervene and that I would not need to say a word on behalf of our son. The Lord moved Gene to allow me to go, and he, Erma, and I left the next day for eastern Texas.

When we arrived in the small Texas town where Dennis was being held, we discovered that the other youths would be returned to Virginia without being tried and that Dennis, the only adult, would "take the rap"—as Gene put it—for all four of them. Both we and Bob's parents realized that Bob had been the instigator of this entire scheme and that Dennis had been manipulated by the smooth tongue of his friend. That did not excuse Dennis. He was still guilty, but it hardly seemed fair.

This injustice aroused Gene's anger. It accomplished what no words of mine could ever have done. He took on single-handedly the justice system of that eastern Texas town.

The Lord undertook remarkably for us in Texas, the most significant example in my eyes being the change in Gene's attitude toward Dennis. Gene talked to the injured parties (the store owners whose establishments the boys had entered to take food). He met with Dennis's court-appointed lawyer, who told us that because Dennis had entered two places in one night, he would automatically receive a penitentiary sentence.

In his early days of employment with the state, Gene had worked with prisoners who were released from confinement and were permitted under guard to assist with road construction. Gene knew what prison does to those who go there. He could not face this future for Dennis.

We met with the sheriff, who told us anyone who had traveled as far as we had "deserved to be heard." This officer talked to Dennis in our presence like a Dutch uncle. "You have good parents," he said firmly. "You don't have to run away. They'd do anything in the world for you." I wondered what Gene was thinking, or whether he was too preoccupied to really understand what this man was saying.

The sheriff sent us to the prosecuting attorney in a nearby town. The attorney received us graciously but could do nothing to help since it was his job to see that Dennis received the punishment he deserved. However, he suggested we drive over to the courthouse and talk to the judge. The district attorney warned, "Don't tell him I sent you!" We agreed to those conditions.

We caught the judge just as he was leaving the courthouse. He sympathized with our dilemma but said he could do nothing but enforce the law. He assured us, however, that our son would be placed with first-time offenders and not with hardened criminals. This did not satisfy Gene. He told the judge he had worked with prisoners, and what one man did not know the next one did.

In speaking with all these persons, Gene poured out

his heart, pleading for our son. He argued eloquently about the evils of the prison system and the injustice of one person "taking the rap" when all four were involved. The Lord answered my prayer about an improved father-son relationship in a wonderful way. I hardly said a word.

With no hope but the promises of God, we left to return home before the trial, bringing Dennis's car with us. As we started south to do a little sightseeing before returning home, I prayed that the Lord would show the judge a way out. Aside from divine intervention, the future appeared very dark for Dennis.

In spite of the seriousness of the situation, that journey south left Erma and me with some good memories. We stopped once in Louisiana to look for seashells along the Gulf of Mexico. Gene happened upon a sand crab, a very agile creature with numerous legs. Watching one cumbersome human being with two legs trying to corner one with eight proved hilarious. Gene finally forced the crab onto the grass where he captured it. He preserved it in rubbing alcohol and our family still has it.

On Saturday, after we had arrived home on Friday, we received a call from Texas. One of the offended parties agreed not to press charges after talking to Gene. Dennis received four years probation and was to make restitution for the stolen goods. As soon as we sent $195.25, he could return home.

The judge with whom we had met gave Dennis his name and address and asked to hear from him. To my knowledge Dennis never did contact him. But I wrote to thank him for his interest and to inform him of Dennis's progress.

Perhaps the tremendous effort Gene put into securing justice for Dennis altered Gene's attitude toward his son. After Dennis came home, he and Gene began talking to each other. Since Dennis no longer owned a car,

Gene took him to see Joe, his former employer, to check on his job status.

Dennis's boss insisted that Dennis seek another job. When nothing materialized, Joe took him back on a part-time basis. This gradually developed into full-time work, a position which Dennis still holds at this time.

When we discovered that a warrant existed for Dennis's arrest due to his failure to appear in court for traffic violations, Gene took him to the police station to turn himself in. Dennis was released on his own recognizance upon his promise to be in court on the proper day.

In spite of the improvement in their relationship, some conflict between Gene and Dennis continued. When Dennis used our car in his search for work, I encouraged him to come home instead of stopping at Judy's home, a habit which irritated Gene. I felt Dennis should show his father appreciation by complying with his wishes. Only after Gene stopped drinking did he and Dennis develop a mutual respect for each other.

Erma, as the only girl in the Crider family, occupied a unique position. Her reaction on many occasions determined whether we would be blessed with a peaceful Sunday afternoon or whether we would experience one marred by conflict. She could, as she phrases it, "jolly" Gene into a good mood or at least a better one by careful bantering or bragging on his meal. She did love his creamed potatoes and has never been able to duplicate his recipe.

Gene refused to discipline the children. Perhaps that explains why he feared demanding their obedience. When he wanted something done, he issued the order through me. He knew the boys would obey me.

One day Gene approached me as I did the laundry in the basement. "Tell the boys to clean the barn," he instructed.

I countered, "Why don't you tell them? They'll do it if

you tell them to."

Gene walked away without replying. A short time later he reentered the basement. "*You* tell the boys that I said they should clean out the barn," he amended; so I did.

The tensions that develop in the home of the alcoholic demand much wisdom. Our heavenly Father promises to give wisdom to those who ask Him for it. "If any of you lack wisdom, let him ask of God, that giveth to all men liberally, and upbraideth not; and it shall be given him" (James 1:5).

Only the teaching of my godly parents saved me from yielding to some severe temptations during my time of straying from the Lord. I hope, in a similar way, my teaching may be holding back our sons from some evils, although they have rejected my values in other areas.

In spite of the wisdom available to me through asking and through the Word, I look back and see areas where I should have done things differently with our children, especially the boys.

Thank God that in all things He does work for good, in spite of our mistakes or errors of judgment!

12. The Matter of Money

The wife of the alcoholic may find herself constantly short of money. This happens because of the amount her husband spends to support his addiction and also because of his lack of sound judgment while under the influence of alcohol.

The techniques I used to stretch the funds available to me are probably outdated and may not be practical in today's economy. I offer them, however, with the prayer that they may stimulate your thinking and bring to mind ideas useful in your situation.

I accepted responsibility for our finances soon after my return to the Lord. It was not easy! Gene insisted upon using two checkbooks, his and mine. He never allowed me to see his checkbook, however, to balance our joint account. Instead, he arrived at a rough estimate of what he had spent. When our bank statement came, along with the canceled checks, I often discovered that Gene's checks totaled as much as $100 for one weekend.

In our area, alcoholic beverages purchased at the state liquor store must be paid for in cash. Gene usually filled the gas tank of the truck and wrote a check for twenty dollars. From this amount he paid the eleven dollars for gas and used the remaining cash to buy whiskey.

One Sunday afternoon when his whiskey bottle became low, Gene drove to a nearby restaurant where he gave another check and bought beer. Gene never used the total amount of those checks for alcohol; I do not know where all the money went. This occurred twenty years ago. The amount squandered today would be much greater.

In the face of the severe financial burden alcoholism imposes on families, how does one make ends meet? How can one stretch the available dollars to cover the house payment and the electricity, telephone, fuel, and grocery bills?

First we must determine to live within our budget. For most of us this means sacrifice, and it seems very unfair. Why should the family of the alcoholic do without just so he can have his liquor? It is not fair, but if we accept the situation as it is, we can say with Paul, "I have learned, in whatsoever state I am, therewith to be content" (Philippians 4:11). The Lord honors such decisions and blesses in unexpected ways.

The first thing I noticed after assuming responsibility for the checkbook was that we no longer bounced checks. The only explanation I can give is that the Lord honored my commitment and intervened; nothing else had changed to cause the difference.

I had grown up during the Depression of the 1930s when my parents were trapped under a load of debt they were unable to pay. We children learned from infancy to make do with what we had. Therefore, my lifestyle with Gene needed no adjusting; I already knew how to pinch pennies and use what was available.

One principle the Lord taught me involving money occurred soon after my return to Him. During our years at the Glen, I sometimes sent the children to our village store with a small list of needed items with instructions to the proprietor that they be charged to our account. I did pay these accounts.

One day I needed a few things—it may have been sugar and jar tops—so I sent the children to the store with the list and note. I recall the note the clerk at the store sent to me. It read, "I'm sorry, Mrs. Crider, but we do not like to charge things."

I am sure I blushed with embarrassment, but after thinking about it, I thanked God for the gentle rebuke. I concluded the Lord meant what He said in Romans 13:8: "Owe no man any thing, but to love one another."

From that day on, if I did not have the funds for something I thought I needed, I managed without it. The key to our financial success was management, and it probably is yours as well.

To illustrate, although I did not have money for jar tops to can peaches, I did have oleo containers that could be used for freezing those peaches. So I froze them. This cost me nothing and also solved my problem.

I learned to stretch our food budget by limiting servings of meat to one helping per person. One chicken made one meal for us. We used a lot of hamburger also, which I stretched by mixing other ingredients with it, then either baked it as meat loaf or pan fried it as patties.

We planted a garden and always had a cellar full of canned fruits and vegetables, in addition to frozen food in the freezer. The children could eat as many vegetables as they liked, but we placed limits on the fruit because peaches, plums, and sugar cost money. We did, however, allow them to eat as many raw apples as they wished, as long as they ate the entire fruit. They were not allowed to discard a half-eaten apple. Waste was a no-no. Apples replaced candy as a snack at our house.

For many years I baked my own bread. When Gene experienced a heart attack on December 10, 1973, however, I could not bake bread and also visit him twice a day at the hospital as he wished. I came across a store that sold day-old bread, and I began buying bread there. I decided I could probably purchase bread as economically there as I could bake it.

For a number of years we attended a grocery auction where damaged goods were sold. We bought cereal, soup, and other goods at below regular grocery store prices. These sales no longer operate in our area, but alternatives do exist. One needs to watch for reduced-cost items, but examine these closely, especially if the product is raw, to be sure the item is of good quality. If you must discard much of the product due to spoilage, you have not saved anything.

I compare prices among brands. Usually the highly advertised products cost more; you pay for the advertising. In-store and generic brands are much cheaper and generally just as good.

I learned to watch where the money went. I received so much criticism from Gene about the grocery budget that I trimmed it to the minimum. I found I did not need some of the things I desired. I got along just fine without raisins, brown sugar, and bacon.

I learned to substitute one food item for another. For example, if potatoes were scarce and money was short, I served rice or macaroni instead. Our children loved rice and gravy.

Similarly, hot cakes and biscuits sometimes replaced bread. Eggs or hot cakes sometimes substituted for cereal at breakfast. I found that if I really wanted to make do, a way could usually be found to accomplish it.

I never purchased lettuce during those early years, but we had green beans and pickles in the basement. The freezer supplied us with lima beans, peas, spinach, and other greens harvested from the garden.

I am not sure whether we saved by doing it, but we bought dried and evaporated milk instead of whole milk in gallon jugs. We could not afford milk as a beverage but did use it on cereal and in cooking. The children also received milk as part of their school lunches.

I cut food costs by using coupons published in the daily newspaper or magazines. We know, of course, that unless these items are ones we normally purchase, we save nothing by using the coupons.

It pays to buy products on sale whenever possible. During the time I baked bread, I usually purchased a twenty-five pound bag of flour when it was on sale. My need for flour and reduced prices on this product, however, did not always coincide!

We cut driving costs by combining errands. I drove about twelve miles to the grocery store. Most of our business contacts were also in the city. Therefore, I tried to do the grocery shopping and take care of business during the same trip to town instead of driving in several times. I generally bought a two-weeks' supply of food when shopping for groceries.

As a girl, I learned to make lye soap, and I have used this skill all my life. Since we had our own lard supply, all I needed to purchase to make soap was caustic soda or lye. This saved us much money over the years. Three cans of lye cost under five dollars, but the soap resulting from the combination of lye, water, and lard supplied my need for laundry soap for almost a year. You cannot beat that!

Lye soap works well only in soft water (rainwater or conditioned water). We used cistern (rain) water for our laundry. Lye soap is an old standby, and I loved the results it produced. Gene's pants and coveralls got filthy from his road construction job, but they came out of our wringer washer looking and smelling fresh and clean.

Although making your own soap may not be practical in today's world, it is one way that I used effectively to hold down costs. Lye is a very dangerous product, and one must exercise great caution in working with it.

Clothing offers a different challenge. My fifth-grade teacher, Mrs. Wagoner, helped me sew the first dress I ever made. From then on I pestered Mama until she taught me to sew. I did a tremendous amount of sewing for Gene and the children.

I learned from my mother how to rip apart a slightly worn garment and recycle it by remaking it with the inside out. The inner side of the garment does not reveal the blemishes that might have been visible on the right side. The colors retain their freshness, and the completed garment often looks new. I made dresses for Erma, pants for the boys, and many coats by using this method.

Today we probably would be farther ahead to visit garage sales and secondhand clothing stores. This would especially be true of the mother who does not sew or has not learned to improvise, or who lacks time for sewing. We might also reduce clothing costs by purchasing less and laundering more often.

It took awhile, but I finally realized there were things I could do to save money, especially where it concerned the health of my family. After rushing Dennis to the hospital with a bout of life-threatening croup, our physician suggested I stock a supply of calcidine, an aromatic black tablet used at that time to control croup. By giving our children the tablet before they developed severe symptoms, I could avoid a major illness.

I still keep on hand a supply of Epsom salts as a first aid remedy for puncture wounds and other injuries. Soaking injuries in an Epsom salts solution has spared us many doctor bills.

Some old home remedies worked fine, such as scalded sweetened milk for simple diarrhea and Vicks for chest colds. Today's remedies may have changed, but the principle still applies: An ounce of prevention is worth a pound of cure.

I learned to prioritize and cut costs when possible. Some bills cannot be reduced. Such simple measures, however, as turning off lights when leaving a room, closing doors between heated and unheated rooms, lowering thermostats in bedrooms, and limiting the use of appliances such as the washer to full loads will help bring down the cost of electricity. Also, using an outdoor clothesline when possible will greatly reduce laundry costs.

Another cent-saver I made use of was the U. S. Postal Service. I reasoned that a postage stamp cost less than gasoline, so I paid the monthly bills by mail. Our local post office was within walking distance, so we walked to the post office. Paying by check benefited us in another way: it gave us solid evidence that bills had been paid.

I learned to be content without such luxuries as ice cream, store-bought cookies, raisins, Sunday shoes, citrus fruit, bananas, toast (no toaster!), chocolate milk, and many other things my grandchildren take for granted.

I needed to learn to accept what the Lord provides. When we pray asking the Lord to supply our need, we do not want to be guilty—when He answers—of saying, "But, Lord, that isn't what I had in mind. That isn't good enough!" We likely would not be bold enough to put our unhappiness so bluntly, but we might find some reason why the thing He provided just is not suitable, or some excuse for why we cannot use it. We might even say, "But, Lord, it isn't the right color!"

This almost happened to me about 1970. I needed dresses badly, and a friend unexpectedly offered me an entire closet full. These garments had belonged to a deceased elderly lady. The colors and pattern of construction all revealed that fact. They just were not my style. But I had asked for dresses, and there they were.

What was I to do? Should I accept what the Lord gave me or was I going to say, "Lord, it isn't good enough. These belonged to an old lady, and I'm not old yet!"

I decided to accept the dresses and thank the Lord for them. After all, if I refused what He provided, what right did I have to ask for more? Besides, only pride would keep me from using those dresses, and pride is sin.

Another important principle for wives of alcoholics concerns credit cards. Many Christian financial counselors would advise you to get rid of them and avoid them like the plague! At one time we carried a charge account with a mail-order company. But this proved too convenient. I discovered I could order bed linens, towels, and jeans for the boys and pay a small amount each month. The bill, however, refused to diminish as quickly as I thought it should. When I read the fine print, I discovered we were paying 21 percent interest for that convenience. I paid the bill off immediately and have refused to own a credit card since.

I remember one Christmas when money was unusually scarce. I bought one small gift for each child. On Christmas morning Gene opened the front door and discovered a brown paper bag propped against the door frame. It contained gifts for the children. We still do not know whom the Lord used to supply our need, but we thanked Him for it.

Eventually, with the Lord's blessing and direction, we succeeded in opening a savings account. Usually Gene's overtime checks—money earned during snow removal or flood damage repair—went into savings. We kept this account as an emergency fund or for traveling expenses.

I did not use Gene's money to give to the Lord because of the potential for problems. Unless I had funds gathered by my own resources, I did not place money in the offering plate.

This principle of giving seemed right to me since Paul says, "For if there be first a willing mind, it is accepted according to that a man hath, and not according to that he hath not" (2 Corinthians 8:12). I did not have; therefore I did not give, and the Lord did not rebuke me for it.

13. The Physical Side of Marriage

During the early months of our marriage, when problems rocked our relationship, I recall thinking, *Well, at least I still have sex.* This thought returned to haunt me many times as I wrestled with Gene's alcoholism and what it did to our intimate relationship. Instead of the joy I expected it to be, this area of our marriage became a battleground.

The very nature of alcoholism partly accounts for this. Alcohol is a depressant, and the effects of the drug prevent satisfactory performance. Instead of acknowledging his impotence, the husband immediately looks for a scapegoat. The person most likely to be chosen for this role is his wife.

I think the intimate side of the marriage relationship requires more grace than any other. This is because something that should be sacred and beautiful becomes, in the hands of an alcoholic, an occasion for abuse, lust, and self-satisfaction. He may even use it as an opportunity to punish his wife for some imagined injury or insult.

In such a dilemma, how are wives to respond?

I discovered the Lord's grace is sufficient even for this. Praise His name!

In the earlier years of our marriage, Gene embarrassed me by touching me inappropriately before the children. I reasoned with him and pled with him to stop this, but he continued the practice. After my renewed commitment, his troublesome behavior ended. I do not recall whether I prayed about it or whether the Lord simply took care of it. But other problems remained.

In our physical relationship I found it necessary at

times to say, "No, I'm sorry. I won't do that." Alcohol removes the inhibitions that govern behavior and opens the door to all types of deviant conduct. A mind influenced by alcohol may demand of us things that are against the will of the Lord, things that go beyond "the natural use of the woman." I needed to respect myself; how could my husband respect me if I had no respect for myself?

Personally, I saw no alternative to submission in normal physical relationships, although these were very frustrating when Gene was "under the influence." The best solution at such times seemed to be to cooperate, pray for patience, and enjoy the experience as much as possible.

People react differently to alcohol consumption. After Gene began coming home on Saturday evenings, I soon learned to expect to be kept awake until 1:30 or 2 A.M.

A variety of accusations often filled those sleepless hours. Some of these were partly true and some were false.

Most of these charges stemmed from actions that in a sober, loving relationship would have been welcome, but under the conditions facing the wife of the alcoholic, these actions become almost intolerable. Each of us must seek wisdom from the Lord to discover the solution to these intimate problems.

I found that during these difficult encounters I could avoid problems by remaining silent. If I did not say anything—trying to refute his accusations, for example—I could not say the wrong thing! And if I did not say the wrong thing, I did not have to explain what I had meant to say. Too often I forgot that you cannot reason with an alcoholic.

I cannot say positively that Gene was unfaithful to me. The evidence indicates he was.

Years after Gene stopped drinking, he visited his

physician because of a severe backache. He returned with a note for me, instructing me to check with my doctor immediately. I had never heard of the particular venereal disease for which he checked me. I do not recall the name of the virus, but I did not have it.

I think Gene picked up this disease during the period of his addiction to alcohol. It must have remained dormant or inactive for some time. If he had been unfaithful to me at any time, that activity ceased when his addiction ended.

How does the wife of the alcoholic cope with such heartache? The path I chose may not be the solution for everyone, but I chose to forgive. I stayed with him. For me, considering the end results, this was the only right thing to do.

Even if the wife of the alcoholic does not face infidelity, forgiveness still plays a major role in the physical side of marriage. I doubt whether anyone feels more "used" than the wife of the alcoholic. Alcohol unleashes lust, and the husband's concern is for himself.

I struggled with anger and frustration over this matter until I learned to accept the situation as it was and decided to make the best of it. Acceptance brings freedom because we submit willingly and not because we have to.

We must forgive because an alcoholic is so unlovely and yet so much in need of love. Submitting to intimacy in those circumstances acts as a test of genuine love. Only the love of God applied to my heart enabled me to do what my old nature cried out against.

I could control my responses to Gene's behavior, but one side of this problem I could not overrule. Erma slept in the room directly above our bedroom. An open stairway led up to it, allowing an unrestricted upward flow of voices. She never understood what our differences involved, for which I am thankful, but she did cry silently many times because of Gene's abusive conduct toward me.

The only method of coping with the frustration of the alcoholic's sexual aggressiveness is in cooperation and in prayer. Both are necessary; they complement each other.

In looking back, I wonder how much I could or perhaps should have done differently. At the same time, I have no regrets because of the long hours of sleeplessness. I was, as Jesus said, merely doing what was my "duty to do" (Luke 17:10).

14. There Is Hope

Praise God, "The Lord's hand is not shortened, that it cannot save; neither his ear heavy, that it cannot hear" (Isaiah 59:1). And because we have many promises in the Word of God, we have hope.

Jerry Dunn states in his book, *God Is for the Alcoholic,* that we can do nothing for the alcoholic until we have prayed for him. I agree with this statement.

I concerned myself first with praying for Gene's salvation. The salvation of his soul held eternal consequences while his addiction to alcohol was temporal. Although he broke the alcohol dependency, to my knowledge he never came to faith in Jesus.

Not until several months after Gene broke his addiction to alcohol, did I learn the circumstances that motivated him in this. I discovered what had happened after noticing an unexplained withdrawal of $220 from our savings account. When I asked Gene about this transaction, the story came out.

The crisis that brought about the change occurred during my trip to northwestern Ontario in 1976. One Saturday night, as Gene was driving under the influence of alcohol, he came upon the scene of an accident. Because he had received first-aid training with the state, he stopped to help, and stumbled right into the arms of the state police.

The $220 covered his fine and court costs. In addition, Virginia law required that he enter the newly inaugurated alcohol abuse program. He came through this combination of events free of alcohol abuse, and we thanked God for it.

A variety of Scriptures sustained me during those

long years of Gene's alcoholism. "Thus saith the LORD; Refrain thy voice from weeping, and thine eyes from tears: for thy work shall be rewarded, saith the LORD. . . . And there is hope in thine end, saith the LORD, that thy children shall come again to their own border" (Jeremiah 31:16, 17).

A similar reference counsels us to "be . . . strong . . . let not your hands be weak: for your work shall be rewarded" (2 Chronicles 15:7).

Although I know that Isaiah 54:13 was written to Israel, I'm praying that God may see fit to apply it to our children as well. "And all thy children shall be taught of the LORD; and great shall be the peace of thy children."

One Scripture I pondered offers both hope and a warning: "For he that soweth to his flesh shall of the flesh reap corruption; but he that soweth to the Spirit shall of the Spirit reap life everlasting. And let us not be weary in well doing: for in due season we shall reap, if we faint not" (Galatians 6:8, 9).

Our alcoholic husbands must surely reap for the fleshly sowing they have done, but we will also reap a harvest of blessing "in due season . . . if we faint not." Over the years I wondered about that harvest. In what areas would Gene reap? Would his health suffer? Or would his harvest come through his sons? Could I expect my harvest to include my children? "And great shall be the peace of thy children" (Isaiah 54:13). I am still waiting—and praying—for that fulfillment.

I thank God for my two children who are living for the Lord. My daughter serves as an adult Sunday school teacher at her church and also carries other responsibilities there. One of my sons is an ordained minister, teaches part-time in a Christian school, and also works in Christian publishing. The children from both these families have accepted Christ as they reached the age of accountability. I praise the Lord for His faithfulness.

Romans 8 became especially precious to me during the years of Gene's struggle with alcohol. "If God be for us, who can be against us?" How wonderful! "He that spared not his own Son, but delivered him up for us all, how shall he not with him also freely give us all things?" (Romans 8:31, 32). I cannot add anything to that reasoning; that says it all.

When Gene brought false charges or slander against me, I remembered Romans 8:33: "Who shall lay anything to the charge of God's elect? It is God that justifieth." *His* mercy is everlasting; He knows our frame and He remembers that we are dust (Psalm 103:14, 17)!

As I look back, the ten years during which I struggled alone without the Lord stretch out endlessly. The eighteen years following, however, during which I walked with the Lord, seem short in comparison.

I pray that this book has been a help to you in coping with your husband's addiction. If it has helped you find solutions to your problems and answers to your questions, I will have been rewarded.

"Now unto him that is able to do exceeding abundantly above all that we ask or think, according to the power that worketh in us, unto him be glory . . . world without end. Amen" (Ephesians 3:20, 21).

May the Lord bless each of you and fill you with His comfort and peace.

Epilogue

Strangely, after Gene stopped drinking, I found something lacking in my life. When I analyzed the problem, I concluded that I missed the challenge to God's grace that Gene's addiction had forced on me.

No longer did I constantly need to cry, "Help, Lord!" when faced with an impossible situation stemming from the consumption of alcohol. Nor did I need to say, "Show me what to do, Lord," when a crisis developed because Gene was under the influence. Or, "Help me be patient, Lord," when it seemed I had taken all I could stand.

Eventually other challenges emerged. Although Gene no longer drank, some of the old problems remained. He never learned to openly show love and appreciation, except to the grandchildren. The shared experiences, mostly small things, told me that he loved me. As far as I can recall he never complimented me or thanked me. I used to think, almost bitterly, that at least he could have thanked me for caring for his mother for almost seven years, but that did not happen. My longing to hear just one word of appreciation from Gene moved me to be sure Gene heard such words from me!

I believe our marriage in later years was as good as it could be under the circumstances. I traveled the straight and narrow way with my eyes centered on Christ. Gene chose the downward path with his heart settled on following his personal desires.

Because of this, we did not share too many interests beyond our family. Gene went his way. I went mine. He attended the country music sing and dance each Saturday night; I prepared my Sunday school lesson. I loved prayer meeting and church on Sunday; he liked the county fair. Although Gene invited me to attend functions with him, he did not insist that I go.

After releasing Gene to the Lord when I returned to Him, I did not grab Gene back. That made parting so much easier when the Lord took him May 3, 1990.

Someone has said, "When we have nothing left but God, we find He is enough." I came to that place when I returned to my God in May 1960. I literally gave up everything else, and He has been enough.

The Lord restored my husband and children to me, but since I had surrendered them to Him, they became His responsibility. God has been faithful. Over the years we have lacked nothing and He has supplied every need.